THE 7
AHAs
EVERY
TRAVELER
SHOULD
HAVE

JONATHAN LEGG

THE 7 AHAs EVERY TRAVELER SHOULD HAVE

FIND PEACE, CONFIDENCE,
AND HAPPINESS ON YOUR JOURNEYS

 **TILTED PLANET PUBLISHING**

CONTENTS

Introduction: The call of travel 7

AHA! 1
Your beliefs are limiting you...
but, you need to believe in something. 11

AHA! 2
It's better to go deeper than farther 43

AHA! 3
Tribal otherness is alive and well.
Only reason and connection will save us. 73

AHA! 4
When things go awry, the true adventure begins. 93

AHA! 5
You can't save everyone. 121

AHA! 6

You are going to die.................................. 139

AHA! 7

The best lives are built on service, community,
meaningful choices, and a lot of mess................... 165

Conclusion... 193

Acknowledgements 197

Endnotes 201

About the Author.................................. 205

INTRODUCTION: THE CALL OF TRAVEL

A traveller. I love his title. A traveller is to be reverenced as such.
His profession is the best symbol of our life. Going from - toward;
it is the history of every one of us. It is a great art to saunter.

~ Henry David Thoreau

Do you ever feel like you're living in a cage? The same office, neighborhood, cafes, and bars. They fill your time, but your soul is restless. There is an itch that is not scratched. There is a curiosity that is not satisfied. Maybe, you've had this thought: "*There's got to be more to life.*"

The answer to this restlessness, you suspect, is somewhere "out there." It lies beyond the bubble of your scene. You feel the same call that came to every mythological hero. The call to go on a journey. The call to travel.

Can you believe there was an emperor who felt the same way? He was trapped in his routine of conquest and carnage. Then one day, he hit a breaking point.

Ashoka "the Cruel" walked over the battlefield after his army had massacred an enemy. The bloody scene gave him an existential crisis. He had to step away. He went looking for the answers "out there." Ashoka's journey had consequences that changed the world forever. Just as you could change your world forever by slinging a backpack over your shoulders and hitting the road.

Deep into his travels, Ashoka encountered a gaggle of monks. They taught him a unique set of ideas… a backwater philosophy which hadn't found momentum yet. This philosophy came from another man, who, like Ashoka, had left his privileged position to wander and seek truth. Ashoka was so gripped by this man's ideas that he spread them throughout his extensive kingdom. Ashoka did for Buddhism what Constantine did for Christianity. He created a state certified religion.

Buddha, Ashoka, and every voyaging hero all point to the same truth: There *is* something out there. Something that will transform you, and by doing so, may turn you into a game-changer… someone who could nudge this world, just slightly, in a healthier direction.

This is the central premise of the book: A traveler can improve this world *if* they are paying attention. Transformed and balanced on the inside, the seasoned traveler is able to transform and restore balance on the outside. The biggest problems we face today are global problems. Our fates are entwined. Therefore, the leaders we need are those who understand this planet best—people who have walked its streets, related with its people, and been immersed in its cultures.

Unfortunately, it's possible for a would-be traveler to completely miss this transformation:

❯ You could sleep-walk through a tour bus itinerary, being spoon fed information with experiences so brief and shallow, you'll forget them as soon as they end.

❯ You might fortify yourself inside the tidy micro-culture of a resort or cruise ship, pressure-sealed from the messy realities

beyond, and fill every loose hour with brochure-quality entertainment.

❯ You could backpack around the globe from one grubby hostel
to the next but, in an attempt to see everything, find yourself
constantly on the move and stretched too thin to penetrate
into any real culture.

This book will help you avoid those traps. It will show you ways to
dive deeper. It will give you tips to avoid fatal and unpleasant experiences. If you become embittered by a scam or theft, the positive
transformation may not take root. If you come to see the world as
hostile, you might not feel it's worth saving.

The idea is to approach travel as a method of accruing wisdom, not
passport stamps or Instagram photos. I'm not going to attempt to
put destinations into any hierarchy and answer the old question,
"What's your favorite place?" The deepest insights and epiphanies
might come to you in mundane or challenging situations. You could
have an "aha" moment in a bus station in Sarajevo, a village in As-
sam, or a moving carnival street party in Salvador.

You might disagree with my conclusions or want to add to them.
Fantastic. My goal is merely to get you to look through this lens
with clear eyes and an open mind. When you do that, the world
will tell you something about who you are and what this is all about.
What it tells you is what you must share. It's the message your
community needs to hear. They don't care how many margaritas
you consumed on the beach. They want to connect more deeply to
the experience of life. You, the attentive traveler, gazing into the

world's soul, will become the ambassador of that connection (in both directions).

I left the suburbs of Illinois as an awkward kid with poor grades and low confidence. I was as clueless about the world as a kid who had never left a tribal village in Africa or a rich enclave of Beverly Hills. Curiosity and a desire to explore led me away from the comfortable confines of the familiar. Flash-forward several decades and I've taught English in South America and Europe, worked as an international flight attendant, acted in Asia, and filmed shows that have aired on televisions across the world. Traveling has changed me into a more centered, open-minded, kind, loving, and courageous man. The road has been my greatest teacher. In the following chapters, I'll share with you the lessons it gave me. One day, I hope to hear about what it did for you.

AHA! 1

YOUR BELIEFS ARE LIMITING YOU...
BUT, YOU NEED TO BELIEVE IN SOMETHING.

We speak about losing our minds as if it is a bad thing. I say, lose your mind. Do it purposefully. Find out who you really are beyond your thoughts and beliefs. Lose your mind, find your soul.

~ Vironika Tugaleva

We are put on this planet only once, and to limit ourselves to the familiar is a crime against our minds.

~ Roger Ebert

*A*kshat pulled me aside. He had some dead-serious rules. "I have just one thing to request and it's that you won't be saying the word 'witchcraft' or mention the black magic."

"What if I do? What will happen?" I asked.

"Well, there are only a few of us who will be out there in these forests," he replied, "and you don't know what she might do."

Akshat was the only local in Jaipur who would lead me to the witch's castle. According to rumors, it was hidden in the dense forest outside of town.

The jungle was thick. The worn tires struggled through deep puddles on the steep, muddy track. Our driver recommended keeping all body parts inside the jeep. Leopards roamed the forest and would rip a man off a vehicle if he leaned too far out from the roll bars. Our asses bounced on hard benches as we squinted into the bush, looking for predators.

The vegetation opened up atop a small, barren hill. The summit was life-less. A single dead tree stood adorned with charms and talismans. Squat-ting beside it was the witch's home. It looked like something between an estate and an asylum: a massive, cellblock-style building, rusty bars on *chipped concrete window frames, and a huge metal gate for a front door, chained shut.*

There were no sounds but for the cawing of crows and hoots of unknown birds, hidden in the tree canopy below. In front of the gate lay a concrete slab with an iron stove on top, ashes spilling out. Akshat, in hushed tones, said this is where the witch's guru was cremated. I pondered how a human corpse could have fit inside that small oven. Was it chopped up first?

I jumped out of the jeep with the producer, Sashi De. Akshat reluctantly followed. The jeep's driver did not budge from his seat. I struck the gate three times with a fist and yelled a greeting. There was no answer. Again, I pounded the gate. Akshat quickly retreated to the jeep muttering something like, "She's not here. Let's go." Sashi stood by my side for another minute, and then he gave up. I wanted this one badly, so I tried one more time.

I pried the gate open as far as the chain would allow and wedged my head through the gap. Pigeons fluttered into flight from an open courtyard, giving me a small jump-scare. "Namaste," I shouted. Suddenly, the sound of shuffling feet… An extremely old woman emerged from the building. She wore glasses as thick as Coke bottles. The remains of her original teeth hung in a mouth that was gaped open with incredulity. She unlocked the gate as two more grannies scuttled out from different corners of the dilapidated structure. Instantly, I recognized the main witch. Her eyes were deep set and dark.

The crew came back. We followed her into a room where she bent down, with pained effort, to sit on a cot. I took a seat on the floor beside her. She picked up my hands and read my palms. She assumed that I had come for a fortune reading. Some of her guesses landed and there were a few misfires. Not bad for a very cold read. I began an interview, keeping the questions general at first, but, eventually, I brought up the black magic. How could I not? Akshat tensed up. The lady looked at me deadpan for a solid five seconds, and then announced that the interview was over.

As we got up to leave, she took us through a labyrinth of narrow passages to another tiny courtyard tucked deep inside the massive building. In the middle of the open space was a small shrine for Kali, the fierce goddess. The head witch grabbed a ladle and scooped water from a sacramental bowl. We took it in our cupped hands and then placed it on our lips and heads, as is the custom. She then commanded one of the subordinate witches to guide us out, and she disappeared through a door. We trudged out in silence. I had some regrets about my tact. I blew it with the black magic question.

Just as we were about to exit the building entirely, the underling witch grabbed me by the arm and gestured that I should have a look in a room to our side. I stepped in. Sashi, tragically not filming, followed. Akshat stood ramrod stiff in the passage, refusing to enter.

The room was dark, but light enough to make out a large image of Kali on the far wall. Skulls adorned her necklace, a bloody sword swung in her right hand, and a decapitated head was clutched in her left. Her outstretched tongue was dripping crimson. Against another wall was a small table covered with beads, coconuts, and amulets. A mirror sat beside it. I gazed into it. There, staring back at me, was the Jonathan I'd expected to see. Wait... something was slightly off between the reflection and the way I was moving my face. Or maybe it was just dark. I looked harder.

"We should go," said Akshat from the hallway. "Yeah, sure," I shook my head to clear it, like one does when they stoop down and then stand up too fast.

"Let's go!" he said again.

We walked out. The gate shut behind us. On the drive down we all sat quietly, contemplating our experience. Then Sashi broke the silence.

"There was something strange about that mirror," he said.

"Yeah, man," I confirmed, "I noticed that too!"

Then Akshat erupted. He was furious. "That's because it's the black magic mirror! This room is where they cast their evil spells. You shouldn't have gone in there!"

He went on to explain all the horror that could befall us. We really made a grave mistake! Dark energy was assuredly coming our direction. A curse would be upon me. I felt his perspective knock on a door in my chest, the fear and uncertainty wanted to take root. Mentally, I pushed back.

Yes, Sashi and I picked up something strange from the mirror. It could have been a variety of things. Maybe the scant light was bouncing around that dark room in an odd way. Perhaps, the mirror was warped like the ones you can find in a carnival's fun house. Even if those old ladies chanted curses into the glass, it would be a leap to assume something supernatural was occurring. I was sure of one thing: If I gave this worry any power, it would grow. The witches had spun a certain story inside many local heads, including Akshat's. I had to spin a different one.

Seeing our guide's anxiety, I patted him on the shoulder and said, "Don't worry, man. My good juju is stronger than that witch's black magic."

He seemed to take little comfort in my declaration, but I did. I *had* to believe that. For, if I accepted the opposite, how might it color the coming hours and days? Every time you cross a busy street in India, it feels like a near-death experience. How much worse would it be to add the belief that something terrible was coming for me?

Maybe, Akshat tossed and turned in bed that night, with troubling thoughts dancing like skeletons in his mind. Perhaps he carried a lingering feeling of doom for quite a while. I had a remarkable experience, full of awe and wonderment. I slept soundly, without a worry. The difference between us was the amount of power we had distributed to divergent beliefs.

SPYING ON JESUS

To be fair, I've been in Akshat's shoes before. At one point I was so immersed in evangelical Christianity that I could not seriously consider any wisdom from another faith, nor could I see any nuance or metaphor in the Bible. If God pulled Eve literally out of Adam's body, then that's exactly what happened[1]. Later in life, the

---

[1] Later, I considered that this would mean Adam had two sexes inside him before the extraction of the female part (i.e. He was a hermaphrodite). He also must have lost ⅓ of his weight or more in an instant. Or, perhaps, this could be seen as a metaphor for the beginning of sex. Organisms reproduced asexually for billions of years before evidence of sexual reproduction appeared. Maybe that's the idea?

pendulum swung the other direction. I became a staunch atheist who considered all myths to be complete mumbo-jumbo. Both of these rigid, polarized positions were limiting me. Travel brought me back to the middle. If it wasn't for the mind-opening power of the road, I would have totally missed the greatest travel story I have in my quiver of tales...

Filming throughout India's northern regions, I stumbled upon the theme of Jesus' missing years. As you may know, there is a gap in the Bible's account of his life from about the age of 12 to 30. A small monastery in the mountains near Leh might hold a clue to what happened in this large chunk of mysterious time. In 1894, a Russian adventurer (and possible spy) named Nicolas Notovich was recovering from a broken leg and was given shelter in the nearby Hemis monastery.

One day, as the story goes, the head lama, in a gesture of friendship, pulled Nicolas aside to show him something few had seen. It was an old scroll that told of a young Jesus who came to Orissa, India, to study Buddhism. He was later driven out of the region by high-status priests (Brahmin) for teaching sacred truths to the lower castes (Shudra, Dalit).

True or not, that's pretty damn interesting, right? Would a younger, evangelical Jonathan Legg pursue it? No way! He would be afraid that chasing this story could somehow lead to the loss of his salvation. Certain beliefs needed to remain unshakable, or the abyss of hell would open up to engulf his soul. Fortunately, at this time, I was in a strict atheist phase, so I kept pulling the thread.

Atheism allowed me to chase the ideas, but it wasn't ideal. It prevented me from gleaning their complete value. I couldn't see the nuanced angles. The atheistic lens, like fundamentalism, was too rigid. Not everything is true or false. Sometimes it's both. Sometimes it's unknowable. Sometimes an idea takes decades of contemplation before it will begin to unlock, revealing dimensions we couldn't previously comprehend.

PUNCHING WOMEN

My limiting beliefs affected filming once again in Amsterdam. I met a top women's MMA fighter, Marloes Coenen, at Glory Gym. A sparring match was proposed for the camera.

In mixed martial arts, if you want to wrestle your opponent down to the mat (ideally, below you), it helps to fool them of your intentions. One way to do that is to feint a head punch before you dive for their legs. Obviously, a fake punch can only be sold if the other person thinks it's a real punch. Therefore, you have to really punch them now and then. Herein was my problem.

I was raised to believe that you don't hit a girl. This ridiculous program was running in my head as I was sparring with a professional fighter, who has been punched in the face thousands of times. So, I never threw a real punch. I only made half-ass pretend punches and then dove in for take-downs. Marloes saw my intentions a mile away. She was probably a little offended that I was treating her like some dainty catalog model.

She threw me around the room like a pit bull handles a rope chewy. She punched me in the face. She choked me until I tapped out. In the end, it made for good TV, but I could have felt better about my performance. I'm not saying I would have won, but if you get to play basketball with LeBron, you don't intentionally miss your shots. You'd like to see if you could maybe score one bucket, right? In this case, with Marloes, all I had to do was drop my constructs and assess the situation with a fresh perspective.

For every good story about overcoming my limiting beliefs, there are thousands that I'll never have. The gorgeous woman I didn't approach in that cafe in Krakow because of a belief that any rejection would be painfully soul-crushing (it never is). There was that chance to start a business in Asia. I gave up on it when a little negative pushback came my way. A YouTube channel was a consideration in 2010. It would have been a great time to start building a following, but lodged in my head was this conceit that, as a TV guy, this online platform was beneath me.

THE MOLDOVAN TEA BAG TECHNIQUE

The way we do things is the best way, is a comforting thing to believe. It requires no changes or adjustments. Change takes effort and moves us into uncertain terrain. Yet, no matter how patriotic we are to our flags, or how proud we are of our hometowns, deep in our hearts we know there is always something that could use improvement.

Growing up in a small midwestern city, it was painfully obvious that grade school and high school could have been better. It was also clear that something was missing in the suburban community. We'd wave at the neighbors, but rarely did anyone step off their side of the fence. Where were all the backyard barbeque parties that were a staple of so many TV commercials?

Conscious travel quickly holds a mirror up to our familiar experiences. It gives us something to contrast against our home. Just as you need two points to triangulate your physical location, we require a different culture to determine who we truly are.

I spent one summer working at a kid's camp in San Martino al Cimino, an idyllic little village north of Rome. Lunch was always at noon, and it proceeded in culinary waves of family-style platters. First came the pasta dish, then the segundi, then the salad, then the dessert, then coffee, and finally fruit. This was a revelation. Back home, everyone ordered their own dish (which came with its own sides). Occasionally, but rarely, someone might offer "a taste" of *their* food. It was my food, your food, their food, or her food, but never *our* food.

The Italian process of sharing dishes creates a sense of commonality. We were all participating in the same experience. We could comment on the different dishes as we ate them together. Furthermore, the multiple courses created an interesting conversation flow. If a topic was getting stale, the next dish's arrival would end that subject. If the topic was good, we would naturally pick it up again. The Italian system of eating is a journey that the table takes together.

Consciously traveling allows us to observe and embrace things we might never otherwise encounter. The Italians clearly have a better system of dining than we do in America. A guy in Moldova showed me a simple way to prevent the tea bag's paper tag from falling into the hot water (tie a simple knot around the cup handle). He had a better system that I immediately adopted. In Mediterranean Europe, some folks still take a mid-day siesta from work. They rest, see their families, and recharge. Participating in this practice will make you reconsider the value of a good nap. When the Sufis worship, the faithful embrace each other and dance as one. Once you experience this, you may wonder why you'd ever sit in a pew again.

Some languages have more nuanced manners of nailing a sentiment. "Bon appetite" is flatly better than "Enjoy your meal." "Shouganai" is more concise than "It is what it is." "Joie de vivre" sounds exactly like what it means.

How we treat children and the elderly is also a keen subject to observe on your global travels. Here, in the U.S., we tend to place our parents in retirement facilities. That's one end of the spectrum. On the other hand, there are certain hill tribes in the Philippines who keep the skeletons of their parents in the attic of their huts (so they can continue to consult with their spirits). In the middle, there are a myriad of options to keep grandma and grandpa in some form of community and with various degrees of autonomy. What is best for their well-being? Where would you like to go as life winds down?

DANGER, FEAR, AND BELIEF

Travel will expose you to scary situations. Once we have, hopefully, survived them, the wise move is to separate what is rational and what is not. Did that situation have a hazardous physical component, was it in your head, or was it a mix of both? In this manner, you can let go of any unnecessary worry, yet stay sharp when real danger is present.

I parse fear into three buckets:

- Irrational fear which should not merit a reaction

- Rational fear which should get a response

- Rational fear which needs to be controlled until action is possible

The three witches in Rajasthan might have deserved a little fear while we were in their lair. They could have stabbed us, poisoned us, or had stronger accomplices hidden in that decrepit manor. I did not believe this was likely, but it wasn't out of the question. Anyone who makes a living by putting curses on people must have a different moral compass than I do. It is a grave mistake to approach the world as if everyone holds the same values and principles.

Once we left the witch's mansion and drove back to town, any further fear would have been irrational. Unless the women had hitmen following us, there was no way these old ladies could exert any more power over me. A simple thought experiment can clarify this. You can keep this in your pocket for anything in the "bad luck" or "curse" category of worry.

How is it reasonable to believe a witch's curse (i.e., a negative intention) has more power than the positive intentions I have for myself? Even my most ardent personal intentions (to exercise, stretch, write, call mom, etc.) often fail to happen. If I can't get myself to the gym, how is an old lady, miles away, going to make my heart stop beating? Moreover, if curses were possible, wouldn't brutal dictators drop dead the minute they lost public approval? Jean-Claude Duvalier held a reign of terror over the Haitian population for 15 years. Nothing supernatural stopped him in Haiti... the land of voodoo and dark magic.

On the other hand, I was once in a London pub with a girlfriend. The front door swung open and a group of men came in. They were drunk and belligerent. I could immediately feel their energy from the other end of the room. I've got an American accent and I was with the only woman in the joint. I walked us out smoothly and quickly through a back door before we became an object of attention. The fear that whispered to me, the moment those fellows entered, was a guide to safety. It was not a mistaken cultural belief speaking. This was a signal that even chimpanzees would pick up immediately.

THIEVES ON A BOAT

Sometimes, a traveler needs to listen to fear and say, "I hear you, but not now." Walking down the beaches of Ghana, many moons ago, my friend Chad and I noticed an old wooden ship washed up on the sand. There was a large hole in the side of the vessel. We stepped inside. As our eyes adjusted to the darkness, I noticed there was a makeshift bed in the corner. A young man sat up in it, suddenly aware of us. Then another man was quickly by our side. A third guy shortly dropped down through a hatch from the deck above. I felt the tingling of danger but wanted to give the dudes the benefit of the doubt. We started a casual conversation.

THE 7 AHAS EVERY TRAVELER SHOULD HAVE

"What do you guys do for work?" I asked.

"Oh, we are thieves," one replied.

Now, the fear response wanted to gush like a fountain. We had put our heads directly in the lion's mouth. But the situation was not ideal for a hurried reaction. We stepped into their home. They *were* being cordial. We were surrounded. The right play was to stay friendly. Humans, like most animals, can smell fear. For a predator, it's an odor that triggers aggression. So, we let that topic pass, spoke on other things, told a couple amusing stories, listened with interest, dropped compliments, and casually left. I'm sure they were thieves, but they were also humans who needed to feel understood and respected. By connecting with these guys on a man-to-man level, and not a thief-to-victim dynamic, we managed to have a pleasant conversation and a small peek into each other's lives. Our wallets continued to reside in our pockets.

Here is an example that happened much faster: In central California, I pulled my motorcycle into a shady alley so I could check my GPS. As soon as I stopped, I noticed a gaggle of meth-heads at the other end, about 50 meters away.

"Don't worry. Just keep a loose eye on them," I told myself, pulling the phone out of my pocket and checking my route.

I glanced up a moment later to see a large man strutting towards me with amped up energy. If I had panicked and tried to turn the bike around, he could have closed the distance faster and ripped me off. I had to tell the fear, "I hear you, but wait."

YOUR BELIEFS ARE LIMITING YOU... | 25

I slid the phone back in my pocket, put the bike in gear, and scooted slowly towards the big guy as if to meet him in the middle. I had my helmet visor up and was beaming a friendly gaze. I slowed to almost stopping as we got even, said, "Hi," and then twisted the throttle. See ya!

THE DODGY NEIGHBORHOOD

In the Philippines, I was at the entrance to Manila's most dangerous slum. There was a metal screen door that led from the edge of a freeway, down a staircase, and then entered the community below. I pushed the door open to have an unimpeded view, and it closed behind me. I grabbed the handle to discover it had locked. The only way out was through the neighborhood. I climbed down the steps, a lone foreigner, into the hood. Instantly, an older gentleman approached me to inquire what I was up to. I told him I was curious about the district. He took me under his wing, in the vein of a proud resident, and showed me around, introducing many other folks as we walked. The locked gate was a blessing. My fears had been unfounded this time and instantly evaporated.

I have slowly recalibrated my opinion of "dodgy neighborhoods" over the years. There are many YouTubers who seek subscribers by walking through sketchy districts. The point seems to always be: It's not as dangerous as you think. They are mostly right. But it would be a mistake to think they are not dangerous at all. You might have a .001% chance of getting robbed on any day in the "nice" area and a 1% chance of getting robbed in a dodgy one. "Dangerous" and "safe" are vague words that suggest the probability of violence, but that probability is never zero or 100%.

There are many factors that will increase or decrease your odds of trouble:

- Time of the day

- Clothes and jewelry you are wearing

- How you walk (do you look lost, like a tourist, or as if you've walked this street 100x?)

- Number of people in your group

- With or without the company of a respected local from that neighborhood

Generally speaking, my biggest concern is disenfranchised young men; full of testosterone and alcohol. Encountering one alone is usually no problem. In a group and drunk? No women in their group? Steer clear. For this reason, I don't go into rough neighborhoods at night. That's usually when men gather to get loose and look for trouble. Around 10 a.m., however, this dodgy demographic is usually sleeping or at a job.

DEADLY MERMEN

So far, I'm encouraging you to parse beliefs into the categories: rational, irrational, useful, and detrimental. However, there is one trap that the intellectual traveler can easily fall into, which a child or simpleton would probably avoid.

While on the east side of Mindanao Island, I spent an afternoon speaking with locals about unusual stories. Folks mentioned incidents that had occurred in the mouth of the Cateel River over the span of decades. People had just disappeared in that water.

One man told me that when he was a child, he was swimming in the river with a kid from a nearby village. As the sun began to set, they agreed to get out and go home. When he swam for the shore, the other kid was behind him. He started to climb onto the muddy bank when he heard a splash and sucking sound. Turning around, he saw nothing. The kid was gone. He assumed the boy must have come out on another patch of the shore. That night the parents of that child and the village chief came to his house. The boy had not returned home. He was never seen again.

There has long been folklore that siyokoy live in the mouth of that river. These malevolent creatures are a mix of human, fish, and octopus. They are notorious for pulling humans down into the depths. Have the siyokoy drowned all the children who have disappeared in that water?

If this same river was in Japan, there would be warnings of kappa, or turtle men. There, the locals post signs with depictions of green humanoids with webbed feet, shells on their backs, and an indentation on the crown of their skull (which must stay filled with water when the creature comes to the surface).

PHOTO BY SEHREMIS

ILLUSTRATION BY MASASUMI RYŌKANSAIJIN

A child would hear a warning that such creatures are in the river and wisely decide not to take a swim. However, a guy like me, thinking himself more clever than the superstitious locals, might mutter, "Bullshit," and dive in. The clever traveler must take a beat and consider, "Is this a stand-in warning for something too complicated to explain to kids?" The clever fellow might suddenly find himself in a sneaky current or the jaws of a bull shark. His lost life becomes one more story to add to the lore.

The savvy traveler must distinguish a superstition that is going to limit them from one that will protect them. If I had followed my fearful guide's advice, I would have never met the witches in Rajasthan. This would have been a shame, as it was a truly remarkable experience. Dismissing the fear of black magic, in this case, was the right move. On the other hand, I would not swim across the mouth of the Cateel River. No way. Dying at the hands of a mythical creature is a hell of a way to go, but getting sucked down into a murky undertow is straight tragedy.

THE VOICE IN YOUR HEAD

In his bestselling book, *The Untethered Soul*, author Michael A. Singer has a clever analogy about an annoying roommate who never shuts up. From the moment you wake till the minute you fall asleep, he's got a running commentary on everything, usually with a tint of pessimism. The room is, of course, our skulls.

Some of us have become so accustomed to the incessant chatter that we hardly notice it, like the hum of a refrigerator or the rattle of an old air-con. But, if you played some music in that room, those noisy appliances would compromise the fidelity of the sound. Again, you may not notice it, but if a friend turned off the fridge and air-con, you would immediately hear the difference in the clarity of the music. In the same way, the voice in our heads is pouring cold water over our experience of life. Is there a way to unplug it?

There is a wonderful mural on the ceiling of an obscure temple in Yangon, Myanmar. The artwork is divided into three frames. In one, Buddha is sitting under the bodhi tree, trying to stay centered. In the distance, a demon is tossing fireballs in his direction, undoubtably fucking up his Zen. In the second frame, Buddha is inviting the demon to sit in front of him. In the third, the demon has relaxed in a cross-legged position on the ground. He's speaking his concerns to Buddha, who listens but maintains an unreactive demeanor. This is the key. When you ignore the voice, it throws a monkey wrench into your vibes. When you give it attention, but not the driver's seat, it softens.

An excellent dojo for working with the voice is any kind of high intensity interval training (HIIT). Every week I run up a small mountain, dividing the endeavor into chunks. For each segment, the idea is to go as fast as possible without stopping, searching for the edge of my capacity. What I was quick to discover is that the mind hits its limits way before the rest of the body. So, I dedicate the first portion of the run to just listening to the voice of that chatterbox roommate. Usually, after about 30 seconds of steep running, it starts to pipe up.

"You ate too much today. Better to do this another time."

"You're not in good enough condition."

"You didn't sleep enough last night."

"It's too hot. Maybe come back tomorrow at an earlier time."

It's trying every angle to get me to stop. OK, fair enough. It's not totally irrational. The body wants to conserve energy and do the minimum necessary to meet its needs. It wants to save that energy for an emergency, like running from a predator. It doesn't get the idea of recreational exertion. This is a fairly modern activity in the vast timeline of *Homo sapien* history.

On the second phase of the run, I begin to consciously take control of the narration. I've developed a whole arsenal of mantras.

"I'm Jonathan Legg. My last name is Legg for a reason."

"My tribal ancestors could flow up this mountain like a breeze. I have their genes inside me!"

"The mountain is pulling me up. It wants me on top."

"I'm already at the summit. It's inevitable. The only question is, 'How am I going to enjoy the process?'"

As I recite the more empowering voiceover, I can feel my legs and breath find a rhythm. Suddenly, a kernel of enjoyment is discovered inside the sphere of hardship.

The lessons from the hill, learned in the simple plane of physical exertion, are immediately applicable in all aspects of life. The voiceover track is always being narrated and is always coloring our experience. Are you aware of it?

HIGH-FIVES

"You!" I heard. I looked up to see a man in a top hat approaching with his left hand up. His eyes glimmered and a small smile cracked inside a dark beard.

"Come get some," the guy said as we locked eyes. We walked towards each other over the narrow bridge.

I had made a last-minute decision to come to Lightning in a Bottle, an electronic music festival, in order to grab some footage for a new TV show idea. My team was delayed, so I found myself alone and a bit out of place in this animated environment.

Have you ever entered a raucous bar at 1 a.m., stone sober? This was me walking around LIB. The crowd was full of people who were amped. They'd spent months in anticipation. They knew the lineups and artists. They were pumping tunes in a caravan full of buddies the whole drive over. And there was lonely Jonathan, ambling around like he was on a filming delay, very conscious of being friendless and older. Basically, my belief was, "You don't belong here."

There is a tradition at that music festival of high-fiving people who are walking the opposite way on a bridge. At least 50% of attendees are in on this game, and 10% are adamant about it. As I crossed my first bridge one of the true believers saw my low-energy body language and he singled me out.

"You!" said the man wearing a steam-punk top hat.

"Come get some."

I pulled my hand out of my pocket and lifted it up. It was like a joust of good will. "Smack!" We made contact. And then, "Smack! smack! smack!" The three folks behind him immediately responded to my raised hand. I was suddenly on high-five automatic.

There is something quite miraculous that happens when you receive a high-five. It's almost impossible to not smile. A surge of energy streams through you. It's as if the giver is passing you a portion of their positivity or a jolt of their current. In fact, scientific studies[2] have shown that this kind of touch reduces feelings of threat and promotes trust and cooperation. It releases the feel-good brain juice oxytocin and reduces the stress chemical cortisol.

That man's decision to slap my hand completely changed my state. Suddenly, I felt like I belonged at the festival. I committed to high-fiving everyone who would accept it on every bridge I crossed.

The high-five is just one example of a rapid state-changing technique. Our beliefs usually drive our states. The state then enforces the belief. It can be a vicious circle when things go south. I had a belief that I didn't belong at the festival because I was alone, unprepared, and too old. This slid me into a state of feeling awkward and out of place. I imagined everyone thinking, "What's *that* guy doing here?" Perceiving the environment through this lens made me believe, even more, that I did not belong.

Often, it's easier to break this cycle by changing your state than by examining your thoughts. Once the state changes, the false

---

[2] High fives motivate: the effects of gestural and ambiguous verbal praise on motivation Bradley J. Morris, Shannon R. Zentall

belief becomes evident. Plunging into cold water, dancing in your living room, meditation, and a drag off a joint could all serve as state changers. What makes a high-five special is that it doles out equal benefit to the giver and receiver. It's a double state changer. Whenever someone shares with you a bit of good news, or a hiker summits a hill where you are standing, raise your hand up and give them some. You'll get some back in return.

THE BELIEF TREASURE BOX

We have not even to risk the adventure alone, for the heroes of all time have gone before us. The labyrinth is thoroughly known; we have only to follow the thread of the hero-path. And where we had thought to find an abomination, we shall find a god.

~ Joseph Campbell

On September 5th, 1977, Voyager 1 was launched to explore the far reaches of space. Onboard, there is a gold-plated audio/visual disc designed to be retrieved by aliens. It's a message from us to conscious beings farther down the space-time continuum. If someone or something in the future were to play it, they would hear greetings in various languages, listen to sounds of earth's wildlife and natural phenomena, jam to global tunes (including Mozart, Louis Armstrong, and Chuck Berry), and view photos that represent our experience here on earth[3].

---

[3] Content of the golden record: https://voyager.jpl.nasa.gov/golden-record/whats-on-the-record/ "Voyager Golden Records" can also be found on Spotify. Want a fun evening idea? Get yourself into a cosmos

We had an impulse to send this information forward. Is it possible that this was not the first time humans had such an idea? Even before language evolved, did our ancient ancestors not draw images on cave walls? As we evolved in our skill as storytellers and artists, perhaps these crude cavern drawings became more refined. Maybe they turned into statues and, as language developed, fables. Valuable and complex ideas were packaged in metaphor in order to send their message, like the golden records, across the vast expanse of time. Perhaps, in your travels, you may have noticed these transmissions.

Buddha sitting under the tree, Jesus on the cross, Hercules' trials, the Garden of Eden, the Eleusinian Mysteries, Brahma/Visnu/Shiva and the cycle of existence, Eshu and the trickster in all its incarnations. The tourist sees the photo opportunity. The conscious traveler will eventually determine that there is something here to ponder and unpack.

But... we know so much more than those ancient, crusty souls! What could they offer us that we couldn't Google with the super-computer in our pocket? It's true that collective human knowledge has skyrocketed. It's also been splintered. Everyone holds a fraction of the puzzle, but nobody has the complete package. Could you, with the assistance of your neighbors, make an iPhone, or even

---

state of mind, perhaps even dress up, and then sit in the dark and listen to this playlist as if you were aliens recovering the disc in a distant galaxy. Then, to extend the game, you could decide what you would put on a new golden record if given the chance. If you were the aliens, how would you respond to the Earthlings - what would you say and how would you get the message back?

a pencil? Could your neighborhood survive off the land if the grid collapsed? Beyond survival, how synced up is the average urban citizen to the rhythms and cycles of nature? What benefits to our health, emotions, and mental clarity might we be suffering, unconsciously, by being out of sync? How tuned in are we to the long patterns in history? How might we be repeating them?

MEN PUSHING LEATHER BALLS

Thousands of Los Angeles Rams fans hugged each other in jubilation after the team won the 2022 Super Bowl. These people would not have displayed this kind of intimacy with each other a week earlier. The fraternal feelings required a shared identity. To what, exactly, were they identified during the Super Bowl?

Strip away the narrative and it's just guys pushing a leather ball up and down a field. It means nothing on face value. However, as of this writing, New York Governor Kathy Hochul is poised to give the Buffalo Bills 850,000,000 dollars in taxpayer funds to build a new stadium. This is money that could be used to treat pressing problems in the state, like addiction, homelessness, mental health, basic infrastructure repair, etc. Why allocate all that cash to watch men move a leather ball up and down a field? In the words of a Bills fan, it "goes to our identity… It's part of our local psyche." In other words, there is a story that's been constructed around the simple endeavor of moving a leather ball. It's the story, not the physical reality, that carries the weight. It's the narrative which is worth all that money and emotional investment.

This points to an important truth about us. We live in both a physical world and a world of narratives. Those narratives serve to tell us about who we are individually and in community. Perhaps you're a Rams fan, a Methodist, an Angelino, a surfer, a gamer. Or maybe you are a Brazilian, a Deadhead, and a libertarian. It's worth questioning how you got these identities and how well they are serving you.

"Who am I?" is one of the most important questions I have ever asked. I ask it all the time. The answer, I believe, will determine much of the course of my life and the satisfaction derived from it. It's a question that commercial and political interests will be happy to answer for us, if we don't answer it for ourselves.

UNPACKING THE MYTH

As you, the global traveler, are exposed to more and more cultural myths, you may ask yourself the following: "Are there some common themes in these stories?" Joseph Campbell is credited for describing the commonalities of the "monomyth" in an easy to digest cycle called "The Hero's Journey."

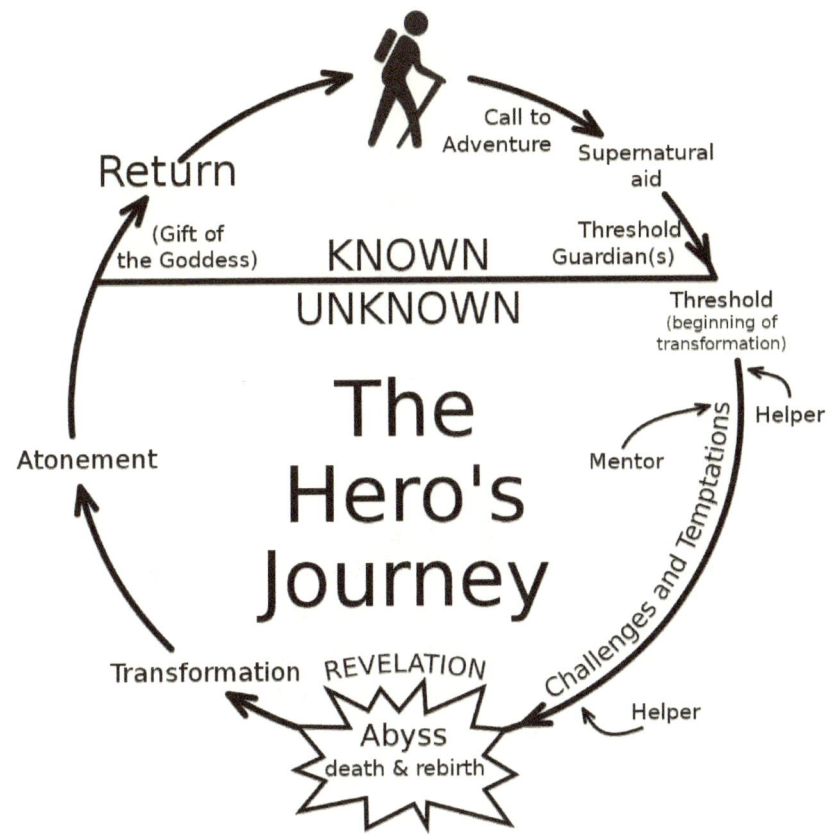

I highly recommend Campbell's seminal works *The Power of Myth* and *Hero with 1000 Faces* to fully grasp these ideas. I regularly revisit these books as a tool for improving my personal story (or myth). Here are some important details I've gleaned from these works and my own contemplation:

❯ You are the hero described in every story, or, that *could* be you. The story has no utility otherwise.

- To self-actualize you must die to a small self with petty interests, and be born to a larger self with more meaningful goals. Ideally, this resurrected you will no longer prioritize personal gain, but will dedicate yourself to a community. The new you will have a deep desire to serve.

- The Hero's Journey is not a once in a lifetime occurrence, but can happen over and over. The same goes for enlightenment.

- Life means nothing and everything at the same time. It's a tragedy and a comedy. It's dirty and, simultaneously, radiating with the divine.

Our ancestors are speaking to us right now. We need their message more than ever. Our attention has been divided and parceled. We have lost connection with each other and to the natural world. History's myths, philosophies, and stories can fill that gap and hitch us back to our roots. They are the narrative and collective wisdom of humanity. They are our story.

Ponder this:

- Can you think back to opportunities you missed due to limiting beliefs?

- Is there something in your life, right now, that is creating a fear response? If so, how could it be divided into the buckets of rational and irrational? Is it something that you could dismiss, should act on right now, or wait to take action on?

- What are some aspects of life that you've seen done better on your travels? How have you incorporated that into your scene back home?

- If you were to sit down tonight and write a page about your story, what would you write? Who are you?

You, the experienced traveler, will first notice how other people are hindered by their bad frames. Eventually, your awareness will turn inwards, and you will begin to see the myriad of your own limiting beliefs. The myths and symbols that once only served as entertainment and photo ops, will become rich sources of contemplation. They will assist you in the process of creating an empowering narrative about the world and your place in it. Conscious travel is a process of continually waking up to a more confident, loving, and understanding perspective.

AHA! 2

IT'S BETTER TO GO DEEPER
THAN FARTHER

....

Everywhere means nowhere.

~ Seneca

*I*would have missed the demons and monsters if I hadn't slowed down. They whispered to me in the stillness of an open schedule.

After we forgot most of our gear in Manny Paquiao's gym, I was left with a free afternoon to explore. This led to visiting a church that had a famous statue of Jesus on the cross. I invited my cameraman, Dante, to come with me.

To enter Quiapo Church, in Manila, one must pass through tiny alleys full of fortune tellers, mystics, and witch doctors. Inside, a clutch of faithful Catholics knelt in front of the wooden pews with their hands clutched in prayer, their eyes gazing towards the statue above the altar, and their lips muttering pleas for a miracle. This particular depiction of Jesus on the cross, known as the Black Nazarene, has a reputation for doling out supernatural assistance.

Once we got inside, I decided to say a few things to the camera about the scene. It never hurts to have extra footage. As we began to roll, an official came up and stopped me. He said I needed to go to the church office to get permission. Seemed like a hassle. I almost didn't go. That would have been a shame as it opened the door to an entirely new episode.

There were plaques on the high white walls of the office.

DEPT OF PRAYER - ROOM 104
DEPT OF CHARITY - ROOM 207
DEPT OF WORSHIP - ROOM 230

Over 20 divisions of holy service were classified on these little wooden signs. None of them seemed very riveting, but it got my little hamster wheel spinning. Could there be any secretive offices not advertised on the wall? When I shuffled to the front of the line, the question was ready.

"Hi. I'd like permission to film the Black Nazarene statue. And... would you happen to have a department of exorcism?"

"Yes, we do," said the clerk, nodding solemnly. Then, on request, he slid me a piece of paper with the address.

That slip of paper, and some patience, led to a whole new, unplanned episode. I interviewed an exorcist, investigated a case of mass demon possession, and looked into a recent slew of attacks by a vampire-like monster called a manananggal[4]. Doing this on the fly required a lot of driving back and forth on the same island. That allowed me to see patterns. For example, every small town had advertisements for recent beauty pageants. Again, the decision to stick around and pay attention allowed me to go deeper. Within a week I was hosting the first ever *Miss Road Less Traveled* beauty pageant.

---

[4] https://youtube.com/playlist?list=PLQiqNpuopPINmDd1-5D7C I7PnOgvWy88g

When I was a young backpacker, I wanted to jam it all in. I "did" the Baltics in ten days. I'd burn the miles down in SE Asia, staying in a town for the minimum time necessary to tick off the *Lonely Planet's* recommendations. With that location "done," I'd be off to the next destination. Nowadays, this instinct is on global hyperdrive, with tour buses stopping just long enough for everyone to spill out, snap a picture, and load back up. Is this driven by a capitalistic impulse to accrue experiences as possessions? Is it a desire to quickly build a travel resume to impress others? Could there be a FOMO[5] restlessness at work?

The obvious rub to this rushed style is that the traveler moves like a stone skipping over a lake. Skimming across the surface of destinations, you don't invest enough time to build lasting relationships. You can't really get to know a city's soul. In the quest for more, you are left with less. Indistinct memories of landmarks, museums, and restaurants will fade fast. You can say, "Oh, yeah, I've been there," but you have no entertaining story or in-depth information to share with others. The value you had hoped to accrue goes missing. The "well-traveled" status you desired is so thin a veneer, it scratches off the moment it's questioned.

The solution is an unheralded recommendation: Slow down and go deeper. Let go of the demanding itinerary. Rent a place in a local neighborhood. Attempt to make one or two friends. Transition between the world of tourists and the sphere of locals.

---

[5] Fear of missing out.

Consider a few of the obvious reasons that deeper is better than farther.

❯ The deeper traveler (DT) is drinking better coffee and eating better food than the farther traveler (FT). DT has the time to search around and find the best spots. There are more chances, on random walks, to stumble into serendipitous finds. The DT picks up tips from locals they see day after day.

❯ The DT is spending much less money than the FT. Transportation is one of the biggest expenses in travel. A walk costs the traveler nothing, yet it can reveal just as much novelty as a costly plane ride. Moreover, the DT often figures out a way, through growing contacts, to get housing at local prices. They get invited to stay at new friends' vacation homes and crash on couches. They can stockpile groceries and cook for themselves. They have time to figure out local transportation routes. The deeper a traveler sinks, the cheaper it gets.

❯ The DT finds the niche scenes in a city that take a while to uncover. Certain subculture gatherings are only learned by word of mouth. It takes time to meet the people who can get you into the punk scene, the hardcore trail runners, or the BDSM crowd. In London, I wanted to join a wicca ceremony; but the members of that community are, justifiably, cautious about who they let into their circle. It took a few days to find a guy, a few more days to arrange a meeting at a cafe (so he could assess my character and intentions), and a few more days to wait for the next gathering. With technology it's becoming easier and faster to gratify our appetites and interests, yet much of the good stuff still takes time to manifest. Only the deeper traveler has that time.

CAVEMEN, COMMODIFICATION, & EFFORT

In recent decades, the core philosophy behind travel has been sub-verted and cheapened. When great ideas become overly organized and commodified, they often lose their original juju. The travel in-dustry promises the goodies for minimal effort—if you only pay the financial price and give them the power to do it all for you. Part of the seductive appeal of this offer is how it plays to an ancient pro-gram running in our brains.

Observe a long plane journey that has just ended. Spilling out into the concourse are hundreds of passengers who have been trapped in a seat for an unnaturally long time. Then, suddenly, a choice: stairs or escalator. Why do so many reasonably fit people, itching to move for hours, opt for the escalator? Perhaps it has something to do with our evolution.

As a hunter/gatherer, there was no question of movement. Modern hunter/gatherers walk 6-8 miles per day. Their predecessors proba-bly moved farther. It would make sense to have a program running in the human skull that dictates, "When you have a chance to con-serve energy, take it. You will undoubtedly need that energy later when you have to evade the lion or hunt the gazelle." But, in today's world there is hardly ever a moment where a reserve of energy is critical, nor do we ever come close to tapping our energy reserves completely. The escalator leads to a moving walkway, which takes us to the shuttle, which stops at the car, which leads to the living room couch. The program in our head that says, "conserve energy for later," no longer serves us in the modern world of convenience and ease. There is no later.

In most of the world there can be found a spiritual monument atop a mountain. Almost always, there is a foot trail leading up. That is how the pilgrims and devotees, for centuries, made their ascent. If, however, a road also arrives at the top, there is not a tour bus in the world that wouldn't take it. In fact, these roads are often built for the buses.

A man steps out of a bus, bumbles about, and takes a couple photos. He gets back into the vehicle. He feels nothing especially profound. Perhaps, he wonders where they might go next and at what time they will stop for lunch. It never occurred to this man that there was a trail. If he had climbed it, following in the footsteps of many generations before him, the experience on the summit could have been much deeper. Maybe, the monument only makes sense, and only fully opens up, to the soul who has physically endeavored to reach it.

Obviously, many travelers have physical challenges that might prevent them from schlepping up a steep trail. The example nonetheless works as a metaphor for the travel experience. Metaphorically speaking, could it be true that the souls of Budapest, Cairo, and Tokyo will not open up to the one who does not climb the stairs? Whether you are 8, 18, or 80, perhaps there is a subjective level of effort which has a correlation to the depth of the experience you get. If it's too easy, the mind undervalues the experience. Without a sacrifice of time and effort, the gods aren't pleased enough to show themselves.

THE SHADOW TRAVELER

Have you ever read a paragraph in a book that punched you in the gut? This happened to me while flipping through *King, Warrior, Magician, Lover* by Gillete and Moore. The authors explore Jungian archetypes and their shadow sides. For example, there is the role of the king. The king resolves disputes, maintains peace, and brings people together under the banner of a righteous cause. It's the Arthurian ideal. It's the kind of leadership we all long for in this world. As the theory goes, we can inhabit this king archetype and so can our politicians. It's like a stream of energy you can step into. But, you must be willing to step out of it when someone else is better suited to lead.

There is a shadow side to the king. When one conflates their ego with the position, a darker nature appears. That is the nature of the tyrant: petty, cruel, and ever fearful of losing power. Unfortunately, we have plenty of examples of this in our modern world.

Ok… safe subject, but here comes the gut punch.

The shadow lover is described as a cowboy who is continually saying goodbye and riding this horse off into the sunset. He is sure that, just over yonder, there must be something that completes him. He is gathering fragments of experience with the hope that, one day, he will be able to piece them together and make himself whole. The moment he encounters a lover's finitude and flaws, it's time to saddle up. He is in search of the never-ending orgasm which is perpetually just over the horizon.

Not only have I been a shadow lover to many women in my life, but also to many destinations, and several business endeavors. The minute a little irritation with a person, a place, or a process set in, I could grab my passport and cross a border. Problem solved, but the cycle began all over again. What I'm learning is that sticking with something through a little difficulty gives access to another level of the experience. As a mentor once told me, "If you can walk through it, there is often a door on the other side."

WHAT MAKES YOU WALK

As a shadow lover, the stimulus it took for me to walk was very minimal. So it was as a shadow traveler. Here are a few of the things which would have me packing. Do they sound familiar to you?

> **Someone was rude** - There is a bizarre phenomenon called Paris Syndrome, from which, typically, Japanese tourists suffer. The Japanese embassy in Paris repatriates several tourists a year, sending them back to Nippon to recover from this condition. Symptoms include hallucinations, anxiety, delusional states, depersonalization, dizziness, and vomiting. Essentially, Paris Syndrome is the most extreme example of culture shock.

French culture is often displayed, inaccurately, in Japanese media. It's slathered with the overly polite and deferential sheen to which local consumers are accustomed, and iced with a fantasy romanticism about a land of starry-eyed lovers, cobblestone streets, and affable bakers shouting, "Bon-jour" as you ride up to put a baguette in the bike basket. Of course, in reality, many shopkeepers in Paris don't give a rat's ass, and they are certainly not going to shout, "Irasshaimase" (Welcome! Please come in!) when a tourist pushes through the doorway. Like any big city, Paris has its fair share of assholes; but, unlike Tokyo, there is no social pressure to conceal one's misanthropy. So the disparity, from what the Japanese travelers think they will encounter and what they get, literally puts tourists in shock.

O.K., so someone was rude, and you got your feelings hurt. Before you curse the place and book your ticket out, consider this: At a minimum, rude people are giving you honesty, whereas, you have no such guarantee with someone who is being polite. Scammers are very polite. The guy who wants to steal your job is super polite.

Sometimes a coarse exchange could mean you are dealing with a jerk, or someone who has had a recent troubling experience. Maybe, they got a phone call from a relative who just got diagnosed with cancer. Perhaps they just lost their job. Or, maybe, the problem is you. There is a possibility that you need to check yourself. In this last case, the rude person is providing some valuable intel.

When I first visited New York, I thought the people were rude. I had my thin skin chapped a few times. However, sticking with the experience, I learned that folks are just curt, because nobody has time to waste. This understanding stuck with me and served me well a decade later.

I had come to Los Angeles as a hopeful actor. I wasn't booking anything. It turns out that my acting sucked. I was way too big with everything, all show and no real internal feeling. Truth is, I didn't even understand the craft.

To make matters worse, my first L.A. acting coach never gave it to me straight. She'd sugar coat any critique so much that I thought I was on the right path. I definitely wasn't. The jobs still were not coming in. Then, I tried a new acting coach.

Doug Warhit, a New Yorker, stood watching as I began my first scene in front of this new group of young actors. Of course, I wanted to impress them. The hottest girl in the class was in the scene with me. Of course, I wanted to impress her.

I got one sentence into my lines when Doug shouted from the back of the class, "Whoa! Whoa! Whoa! Stop!" I looked up in dismay. "Jonathan," he continued, "you will never get a job in this town if you act like that!"

I felt my face flush red. Rage billowed from my chest. I was humiliated, but, crucially, he got my attention. The rudeness of his comment was, in fact, penetrating truth. It took the blinders from my eyes. I now knew that I needed a complete rework. I had to drop my ego and come to the art of acting as a true beginner. Within a month, I began to finally book work.

The rude guy at your travel destination may have, similarly, given you some gift.

In fact, most people who bruise feelings must compensate by being really good at their craft. I've worked with editors before who were the sweetest, most friendly people. I gave them many chances to get a job done right, despite their fumbling efforts. On one particular occasion, valuable time was wasted by someone who really was not qualified for the job, but you want to cut the nice person a break, right? On the other hand, the jerk is not going to get any slack, so they have to do it well. This principle seems to play out. The editor who is rough around the edges gets the job done. If they didn't, they'd be out of work fast. Of course, it's best to work with people who are both affable and talented, but business is business.

If you have to deal with an asshole, there is an opportunity to learn how to handle these interactions without allowing them to ruin your day. Before we completely dismiss ourselves of any responsibility for an unpleasant encounter, it's worth a quick internal assessment. Was I approaching the situation with kindness and respect? Was I signaling weakness by not holding any boundaries? Did I bungle my language skills and say something offensive?

Putting effort into unpacking these experiences can break us through to new levels of understanding. Walking away, the minute we get our egos bruised, gives us nothing.

You got sick - I was in an Airbnb in Kiev when I noticed a bump on my right testicle. "Fuck, I've got cancer," was my first thought, followed by self-encouraging talk about how I could handle such a diagnosis. Of course, there is an impulse to fly back home the minute one's health goes south. It's natural to want to be closer to the doctor you know, the comfort of a familiar environment, and friends who could support you through the malaise. On the other hand, you are probably stronger than you suspect, health care might be better (and potentially cheaper) in this foreign location, language difficulties can be surmounted, and the experience, in totality, grants you access to a side of the destination most tourists never see.

I had a very memorable time at a Ukrainian clinic. On a table, rolled over onto my side with my pants down, I was communicating to a couple of nurses via a translation app on my phone while they stuck a probe up my anus. We all laughed at the absurdity of our lives merging at this unique moment in time. With the data, a doctor expertly determined that I did not have cancer, but an infection in my urinary tract. He then gave me the right medication that solved the problem. Moreover, the whole experience left me with a life-affirming glow. I put my health in the hands of these people from a foreign land, and they took good care of me.

⊗ **You got swindled** - I got ripped off by a driver in Aswan, Egypt. By the time I realized he shortchanged me, the dude was long gone. Damn, did that sting. I couldn't sleep that night as I replayed the incident and berated myself for not catching the deceit. Getting burned can definitely paint a destination with a dark brush. It was tempting to move down to the next place on my route and physically leave that memory behind me. But, if I had done so, that would be the dominant impression I had of that city. If anybody had later asked me, "How was Aswan?" I would have told them about how I got ripped off. To this day, this is the one memory I have of Panajachel, Guatemala. I didn't want to have another story like that.

On the advice of the hotel staff, I walked down to the office of the tourism police and shared my frustrations. They took it very seriously, dispatching a cop (who looked like an Egyptian Magnum P.I.) to accompany me across all the places these drivers liked to hang out. We canvassed the city. Eventually, in a wide plaza, the long arm of the law came for that shady driver. Boy, did I strut when I walked up to that guy, savoring the approach of justice. In a panic, he returned my money and pleaded for mercy. I told the cop it was all good. I just wanted the cash back. He made the dude sweat for a few minutes, and then we split.

Back at the station, the chief asked if I was satisfied with the results. I reiterated that I just wanted the money. There was no need to give the guy any more trouble. He was now on the cop's radar. I didn't think he'd try that stunt again. The old chief nodded and slid a document in front of me to sign. It stated that I had lost some money on the streets of Aswan and, with the help of the tourism police, that money was recovered. Sounded true to me. I left that police station beaming. I got my cash back, refused to be a victim, and had a fun day touring the city with that cool cop.

The bottom line is that all of these challenging experiences are like a fork in the road. The beaten path is the one of retreat... to run for a safe space or an imagined greener field at the next destination. The more challenging, less traveled route offers an opportunity to push through difficulty and find, on the other side, a more intimate connection.

DEPTH CHARGES

As a traveler attempts to understand a new land, there will be obstacles to sinking deep into the experience. Some of them are as old as Herodotus. Others have only recently emerged, but pose a steep challenge to reaching profundity in our journeys and our lives.

- **The phone** - It should be a surprise to nobody that there is a war for our attention, and most of us are losing it. Have you ever caught yourself doom-scrolling and wondered, "How did I get here?"

During a loose moment at a travel destination, literally the best thing to do is look around and take things in… to soak in the sounds, sights, and vibe of a place. That's why you went there, right? Why would a traveler, sitting on a park bench in Brasov with autumn leaves falling around her, or at a cafe in Assisi in a gorgeous piazza, be gazing down at her phone? Why scroll through two-dimensional, dated, and polished images of life when vivid, raw, three-dimensional life is happening right there? It doesn't make sense. It's not a logical choice. It's a decision your best self would never make. Your best self has obviously been kidnapped by technology. There must be hard parameters in place to fight back. Here is what has worked for me.

▶ **Hard time limits** - The first hour after waking up sets the tone for the day. It's a good time to affirm who you are and what you want to accomplish. Whatever your routine is, the phone or laptop can be a devious intrusion. The second that email, news, texts, or social media are opened, other people's concerns begin to flood the zone. One peek can pull you right out of your center. Start with your concerns first, then open that door.

The hour before bed is a time to wind down and reflect on all you've accomplished, experienced, and learned from the day. It's when the body should be preparing for sleep. Ideally, your head hits the pillow with your soul feeling, once again, centered. In the evening, a peek at the phone does even more than pull you off center. The light from your device is a melatonin crusher.

▶ **An extra step** - In his book, *Atomic Habits*, James Clear speaks about removing steps for habits you'd like to pick up and adding steps for ones you'd like to drop. To get out the door of your hotel for an early morning walk, have the shoes and clothes all set up beside the bed. To keep from looking at your social media while you take that walk, erase the shortcut thumbnails on your phone. Now, you'd have to pull down a search bar and type in the name of the app. That extra step gives the conscious mind time to come online and ask, "Is this really what I want to be doing at this moment?"

▶ **The sabbath** - There is some real wisdom in this ancient religious tradition. If God rested on the 7th day, maybe it's not a terrible idea to give it a shot. Although you could choose any day, I find Sunday vibes are perfect for leaving the phone in a drawer. Saturday is loaded with big plans, events, and expectations. By Sunday, most people have blown their load, and are dropping into a more tranquil rhythm.

The sabbath, to me, is a time to shut off the noise from anything that is not physically present. I don't need to be updated on wars, political situations, and trending subjects. I don't need to know what remote friends and strangers are posting on their socials. I don't need to check the email. All that stuff will be waiting on Monday. With this stream of input significantly diminished, the mind finds more capacity for output. I can give more attention to my friends, to the forest I hike through, or to the creative ideas I'm jotting down into a notebook.

In our modern culture, there is an unspoken mandate to always stay productive. Taking a sabbath feels a bit scary, because it seems like removing your foot from the gas on a busy highway. Won't you fall a step behind the madding crowd? No. You'll discover that productivity actually increases. Turning down the noise allows new thoughts to emerge over every aspect of your life and work. When you return to work the next day, these epiphanies will improve your output.

Many circumstances, for which a phone might seem necessary, can be negotiated the way humans have done for eons. We can navigate without a device. In fact, asking locals for directions is an excellent way to have those micro-encounters which bring texture to a good day. Those locals might have additional info or a friendly side conversation in their capacity. We can find a place to eat without a phone. Again, ask people, or stroll around and see where the locals seem to gravitate. We can set up arrangements to meet a new friend or potential lover without a phone. Writing a number on a napkin, with a little note, carries more punch. The extra step it would take for that person, to later type your data into their device, means something. Effort means something in the formation of a connection. Even better, forget the numbers. "Meet me beneath that statue in the plaza. I'll be standing there waiting for you tomorrow night at exactly 8 p.m." There's no way to reschedule or delay. The time must be prioritized. There is a degree of risk added to the effort. If you both show up to that statue, things are off to a fantastic start.

Trust that what comes to you on the sabbath is what you're meant to experience. There is no need to reach out remotely for more. Let your friends know in advance that, if they want to see you that day, they better plan ahead. Find a natural rhythm to the hours. Navigate as the spirit moves. Journal, play, read, connect, create, and savor the immediate.

- **The itinerary** - It's fun to jot down a bunch of ideas for a new destination. It's worth making a loose schedule. Being married to that list is a huge mistake. You must look at it as a collection of suggestions, not commandments. Too often, I have left a fantastic time because I felt compelled to stick to a silly schedule, as if it were the word of God.

Of course, we want to see it all. There is a natural desire to maximize a chunk of time. As mentioned before, modern culture encourages us to ultimate productivity. Those same work ethics bleed into our travels and steal from us opportunities to be still and to soak in a moment in time. Destinations become checkboxes instead of essays. The list we are left with impresses no one and leaves no solid lasting memories. Better to have one great travel story from just one destination, than nothing but passport stamps from five. Nobody cares about the stamps. Eventually, you won't either.

To combat the draw of an itinerary, we must remind ourselves that it's always just a suggestion. It's always open to revision. Equally powerful is a tip I learned from Rick Steves. Tell yourself, "I'll be back." You can let go of that next place on the schedule, because it will come to you again when the moment is right.

❯ **The hype** - Guidebooks, apps, and webpages can't help themselves. They love to rank attractions, often with a row of stars. Yes, this is where the masses go, but the crowd also prefers *Transformers* to *Todo Sobre Mi Madre*, Tom Clancy to Tolstoy, and a Quarter Pounder with Cheese to a cut of lean meat on a bed of fresh veggies. Do you really want to trundle down the path of the masses? Moreover, the game is often rigged. There is a tourism infrastructure surrounding the bigger sights designed to take your money. Naturally, the brochures and websites will lead you there. They see you as a consumer.

This isn't to say that the number one ranked sight isn't the most impressive thing in town. It often is. Most media would place the Taj Mahal as the best attraction to visit in India. The Eiffel tower ranks at, or near, the top in France. These choices are completely justified. They are architectural masterpieces. The big question is: how many travelers will say, after a long journey through both of these countries, that the best experience they had was walking through the Taj or gazing at the Eiffel tower? Very few.

▶ Hyped attractions are wrapped in massive, unavoidable expectations. Unless you crawled out of a cave, there is no way you haven't heard of the Roman Colosseum. The bar is automatically set high. Anything short of being spell-bound could feel like dissatisfaction. On the other hand, you might be taking a stroll through a town in Abruzzo, when, around the corner, there is a wonderful little museum you knew nothing about. That museum has no bar to clear. It's pure serendipity.

▶ Hyped attractions are usually jam packed with tourists. Shuffling around the Louvre, with the crowd pushing you along, it can be challenging to sink into the art. Perhaps, you would have more fun playing hide-and-seek in that dilapidated medieval castle, sitting above an untouristed village in the French countryside.

▶ Hyped attractions are staffed by employees who are overwhelmed by the numbers they have to handle. They don't have time to sit down with you for a chat. They are not going to invite you for a coffee. They might not even look you in the eye. The people who will give you the most attention are the thieves and touts who gravitate to these locations. Friendliness is hard to trust, as it could be a set up for a sale or a scam. You can't be totally at ease with your belongings.

Contrast that scene with what I found in the Old Mission Church in Kolkata. I noticed its unique architecture from the sidewalk and wandered inside. The main doors were locked, but I kept bumbling around until discovering a dark passage in the back. Stepping in, I met the old, affable caretaker. He invited me to sit down for some tea in his little office, shared some personal details about his life, showed me the room where he slept, answered questions, gave a personal tour of the church, and then handed me a book. You won't find that church on any top 10 (or top 50) list for the city of Kolkata, but it was my favorite memory from my last trip to that city.

> **The attitude** - I had a big shift as a traveler when I changed my focus from *getting* an experience to *co-creating* one. Tourism sells us on this idea that we will feel something unique and desirable at a particular destination.

Come to the Caribbean to finally relax.

Come to Vegas to have your hedonic desires gratified!

Come to Iceland to reclaim that sense of awe you haven't felt since childhood.

Fuck yeah! I want to feel all those things. Yet, by playing this game, a one-dimensional frame begins to creep into the way we see a destination. It's there to provide you with something. Looking at the world through this frame, the traveler is always the beneficiary and the destination the provider. Is that how it really works?

Commodification culture won't tell you differently. Imagine a tourism board pitch, or advertisement for an airline, asking, "Jamaica: What are you going to bring to our precious island and the community that inhabits it?" It would be unthinkable to turn a sale into a moment of introspection. A conscious traveler, therefore, must turn it on themselves.

Consider the number of people one encounters in any given location, from the brief contacts (taxi drivers, servers, baristas, etc.) to the more lengthy (new friends, lovers, professional contacts, etc.). They are all left with an impression of us, and, more importantly, a feeling (or lack of feeling) from the encounter.

Let's create a tale of two taxi rides. In one, the traveler is absorbed in unimportant distractions on their phone. Perhaps, the traveler has an unspoken belief that there is nothing to get from the driver other than his service. On another ride, the traveler throws out a conversation gambit and sees if the driver engages. Obviously, not all drivers want to talk, and there are times when a traveler is so exhausted that they just want to gaze out the window and find some Zen. However, there are some wonderful, deep conversations waiting in taxis. I've learned things from drivers, been inspired by drivers, and felt more of a connection to the zeitgeist of a destination thanks to drivers. I've had interactions that have left us both feeling good about ourselves and the world in general. That's co-creating an experience at the destination. Those are the moments when traveler/local statuses begin to blur. It becomes a conversation between two humans, traveling through life, trying to help each other sort the whole thing out.

When it comes to travel romance, the scene has certainly gone on steroids since dating apps emerged. My god, it's like a candy shop. Both men and women are simply overwhelmed with all the shiny objects. When the matches start piling up, it sure is easy to slip into that frame of taking an experience from someone. But, again, when a certain threshold of sharing and intimacy is crossed, there will be something given as well.

It only requires a little more effort, and a little more attention to pick up on a person's situation. Everyone is, consciously or unconsciously, sharing their hopes, fears, and desires. By the time you part ways with a travel lover, or a travel friend, consider if you've tried to leave them in better condition than when you met them. Do they feel encouraged and invigorated by the encounter, or somehow deflated? How did they leave you? Were you co-creating some beautiful moments to share, or were you looking to simply get something?

BORING!

You leave your home excited and travel to a foreign land with the idea of *stimulation*: sights, events, romances! However, the day comes when you are alone in your rented room, starting at the ceiling. Like a phantom, twin sensations begin to swirl around you: boredom and loneliness.

Alas, in this new age we have a quick way to expel these unwelcome spirits! We yank the phone out like a magic wand. Cat videos, Candy Crush, and Tinder swipes can pull us immediately away from dreaded boredom. But, where are they taking us? Do they induce sensations of pure bliss, meaningful engagement, or Zen tranquility? How do you really feel when you catch yourself in a social media doom-scroll? Happy? Perhaps, if we just sat with the boredom, something might have appeared on the other side, just as you must sit with the problem before resolving it or hold some discomfort in order to get a proper workout at the gym.

Sitting at an outdoor cafe in Tbilisi, I felt boredom kick in. Next, the impulse to reach for my earbuds and phone. I paused a beat and observed the urge. It turns out, reaction was not mandatory. I recalled the words of Sam Harris who said, "boredom is simply a failure to pay attention." I tried to wake up to what was happening…

"How does the sunlight feel on my skin?"

"How does the slight breeze feel on my face?"

"Is there a scent in the air? Ah, yes… Jasmine!"

"How many different sounds are in my environment?"

"Who are these people walking past me down the sidewalk, and what can I intuit from their gait and expressions?"

The boredom was a cue. It was a signal to wake up to the moment.

Later that day, back in my Airbnb, a wave of loneliness washed over me. I was planning to grab a beer with a new friend, but he texted to reschedule. I examined the feeling. Could I be OK with my own company tonight? I grabbed a notebook and stepped out the door. The night walk led me to some ancient ruins. Perched up on the crumbling walls, the sensation of loneliness transformed to a space of introspection. I scribbled three pages of notes, full of appreciation for life, plans for the future, and affirmations of values. The loneliness was, in fact, a signal to recenter.

The next time you feel loneliness or boredom, could you leave the phone in your pocket and try to sit with it for just a while? Is it trying to tell you something?

THE TRAVEL SUBMARINE

Despite the myriad of obstacles, there is one solid way to plunge down into your travel experience: intention. On the road, as in life, possessing a plan, even a ridiculous one, gives you purpose. The plan is always amenable to change, of course, just as the captain of a ship adjusts the heading throughout a journey. The intention is like a rope which can pull you out of tourist traps. The right mission will lead you to places where you will meet genuine locals and have unique experiences.

Here are a few missions I've pursued:

> Writing a guidebook to the Baltic states: Researching the content had me popping my head into every bar, restaurant, hotel, and attraction in Tallinn, Riga, and Vilnius. I never published the book (it got out of date before I could complete it), yet, the journey it took me on was well worth the endeavor.

> Riding a tandem bicycle around Hanoi, picking up a variety of passengers along the way. I was later able to sell the bike and recover most of my money.

> Producing a short movie in Romania for 700$ (including casting, wardrobe, logistics, and salaries for a make-up artist and actors).

Here are more silly ideas for future trips:

- ❯ Throw environmentally-friendly paper airplanes off the 5 highest peaks at your travel destination. Jazz it up. Design the planes with names of friends, sentiments, or worries you'd like to let fly.

- ❯ Instead of just going to Vegas to party, take the Old Mojave Road[6] to Vegas... then party.

- ❯ Find the best croissant in Paris, the best cappuccino in Rome, or the best taco truck in Los Angeles. Put an interesting spin on the mission by forbidding the use of the internet or apps in your search. All direction and advice must come from locals.

- ❯ Many European cities (e.g. Florence, Belgrade, and Yerevan) are loaded with fountains that deliver water from ancient aqueducts. As a unique way to explore the city, one could journey to a handful of them, taste the water, and rate the experience. Judge each fountain by a few metrics: taste, beauty of the environment, and design of the fountain. Many locals in Rome claim the water at the base of the Spanish Steps is the sweetest in the city. Would you agree? Which one would you choose?

- ❯ Buy a traditional outrigger boat in the Philippines and sail it to different islands. My buddy accomplished this for about 3,000$. Alternatively, one could buy a boat or raft in several countries and navigate down a river. Sell it when the journey is done.

---

6 "Road Less Traveled in Mojave Desert" - https://www.youtube.com/watch?v=UGkB8_0boNA

❯ Look for a missing treasure[7] or into an unsolved mystery. The Lost Dutchman's Mine hasn't been officially found. There is an old horse-drawn wagon full of whiskey buried somewhere under a dune in Nevada. General Yamashita dropped a heap of booty in the tribal hills of Luzon as he retreated from Allied forces. Only a portion of that has been found. The chupacabra, El Dorado, and Arc of the Covenant may still be out there. Will you find them? Probably not. Will you have a unique adventure in the search? Hell yes!

Ponder this:

❯ Have you ever been a shadow traveler? Did you walk away from a destination when you could have gone deeper? Why did you move on?

❯ Is your phone helping you or inhibiting you from really connecting with your travels? If you were to set some parameters around it, what would they be?

❯ Can you think of a silly mission you could do on your next trip?

You, the introspective traveler, have come to realize that profundity has more value than distance. There will always be another horizon, but a life chasing ahead will leave you spread so thin that it's as if you were never there. There will be frustrations that test your capacity to stay in the game. But a challenge surmounted on the road brings you into more intimacy with a destination. It also improves your confidence to handle trouble away from familiar comforts.

---

[7] "10 Amazing Lost Treasures No One Can Find" - https://listverse.com/2014/10/19/10-amazing-lost-treasures-no-one-can-find/

Like the arm floaties a child wears in a pool, there are obstacles that can prevent a traveler from plunging deep; but with the right awareness, you can overcome the things that would pull you towards the surface.

Ultimately, nobody cares how many stamps you have in your passport, but everyone can benefit from the unique wisdom spread across cultures and minds. The best way that you, the traveler, can secure that treasure is to stick around long enough for a destination to unlock and the people to open up. It's better to go deeper than farther.

AHA! 3

TRIBAL OTHERNESS IS ALIVE AND WELL.
ONLY REASON AND CONNECTION WILL SAVE US.

Reason is always weak, where prejudice is strong.
~ Norm McDonald

*Travel is fatal to prejudice, bigotry, and narrow-mindedness,
and many of our people need it sorely on these accounts. Broad,
wholesome, charitable views of men and things cannot be acquired
by vegetating in one little corner of the earth all one's lifetime.*
~ Mark Twain

We have a big problem right now. Can you feel it? We are losing the ability to speak in a common language. In the current climate, we all have our personal sets of beliefs and facts, which must be protected from challenges. Perhaps, the world is changing so fast that we are all compelled to cling to tiny allegiances like floating devices clutched in stormy seas. Or maybe, we are actively being divided by technology gone awry, or powerful interests that want to keep us confused and in fear. I'm not sure. What I suspect is that this current direction will not lead to a happier, healthier future for our descendants. There is one that could. It's an understanding that any conscious traveler has already glimpsed. I'll use two rather extreme travel stories to illustrate my point. One story almost ended in my personal destruction. The other story almost ended in the death of us all.

I've traveled to Leh, a state in the far north of India. It's where all the Tibetan refugees fled to when the PRC set out to destroy their way of life and bring in Han settlers (A move very reminiscent of the American "Manifest Destiny" expansion to the west). The landscape is full of gorgeous monasteries tucked into sheer cliffs. The main city of the region sits at about the lowest altitude in the state – 11,500 feet.

Every monastery has its own curiosities, but Hemis is linked to one of the most interesting stories you'll ever hear. It's either one of history's best hoaxes or a secret that the establishment desperately wants to bury. This is where, the previously mentioned, Nicolas Notovich claimed to have seen a scroll documenting Jesus' missing years. I managed to arrange an interview with a monk to follow up on Nick's claims, written more than 100 years prior to my visit. During my conversation with the holy man, I warmed him up with a few softball questions, and then, once we had a little flow going, I threw him the question about the manuscript (allegedly called "Life of Saint Issa, Best of the Sons of Men"). There would have been a hundred ways one could argue against this story, but curiously, the man dodged my question.

I asked, "Is there a scroll in this monastery that documents the life of a young Jesus?"

He answered, "It's impossible that Jesus was here because the monastery is not that old."

I let it go. I regret this. I wish I had pressed him just a little harder, but it did seem like we were on thin ice. True or not, they want to stay focused on Buddhism, not this story. We moved on to other subjects to complete our travel show episode. However, before we left the region, I picked up on the Jesus thread again.

In the town of Srinagar, located in the disputed Kashmir region, there is a mausoleum. I learned that there was a man buried there in the first century A.D. His name was Yuz Asaf. Over a thousand years later, Islam arrived in the region and the structure was turned into a mosque. A Muslim holy man was buried above this first man. The Muslim's corpse is apparently oriented towards Mecca. Yuz Asaf's body is aligned to Je-rusalem.

You probably see where this is going. Buckle up as we now dive into the 'Swoon Theory.' According to this hypothesis, Jesus did not completely die on the cross, but rather fell into unconsciousness, or a coma. He was then carried to the secluded tomb where he was treated and revived.

There are some interesting arguments for the idea. Most people who have been crucified took days to succumb. Jesus spent six hours on the cross. The Roman soldier in charge of guarding the scene publicly declared, "Truly this man was the son of God!" (*Mark 15:39*). Does this imply he was a believer/ally/follower? Maybe he pulled Jesus off the cross when he dropped unconscious? The medicines Nicodemus brings to the tomb (myrrh and aloes) are more aligned with treatment than burial.

Still following this theory, Jesus is resuscitated in the tomb. He sincerely thinks it's a miracle. His devotees believe it's a miracle. Nothing was disingenuous about their feelings or beliefs. They also, undoubtedly, believed one more thing: They had to get out of Dodge. The Romans played hardball with their enemies. If they caught Jesus out in public again, he would have been chopped into pieces.

So, what to do? Where to go? To the west was the entire Roman Empire. To the east, accessible via the Spice or Silk Routes, was a country of religious tolerance, outside of the Roman Empire's control: India. Perhaps, Jesus remembered this place from his youth.

These are all very controversial ideas. How could I not pursue them?

The producer, Sashi De, and I arrived in the town of Srinagar, hired a taxi, and asked the driver to take us to the shrine. He stopped a few blocks short. The neighborhood had become quite dangerous, he intoned. He didn't want to be involved in any trouble. So we got out and walked.

We arrived at the shrine and began filming. Suddenly, a man yelled and came running up to us.

"What are you doing here?" he asked aggressively.

I explained that we were filming a little piece for a travel show, but kept the specific subject matter vague.

"No. Get out of here," he said flatly. Now, a couple friends of his trotted up to the scene.

We began to walk off. I whispered to Sashi to get in front of me and film as we left. I gave the synopsis quickly as we moved. The men saw what we were doing and ran up on us again.

The next moments are still a bit of a blur. Men kept arriving. The circle that surrounded us grew and became more and more agitated. Have you ever seen a hive of bees as it becomes threatened? There is an audible shift in the energy of their buzzing. This is exactly what I witnessed as the group of young men began to morph into a mob. A desperate fear sprang from my chest. We were in mortal danger.

There was no escape. There were no police or army in this neighborhood. We were at the mercy of a group of men who were suddenly not viewing us as fellow humans, but rather as "the other." The other can be a container for all of one's frustrations in life. The other can hold everything that is wrong with the world. The destruction of the other could perhaps, for a moment, set things right.

Suddenly, our taxi driver jumped between us and the swelling mob. He spoke quickly and emphatically. It was clear he was pleading for peace. Perhaps, he was cherry picking verses from the Quran that supported non-violence. In the middle of his frantic rant, he looked at me, over his shoulder, and commanded, "Get in the taxi!"

There it was a few meters away. Salvation. I ripped a few hands off of my clothes and forced my way into the car. Sashi followed. The driver, still pleading, managed to hold back the dark tide until he too could enter the car. We drove away with voices yelling and hands pounding on the vehicle. The first few blocks passed in silence. My hands were shaking. Then the driver spoke as he looked at me in the rear-view mirror.

"You are very lucky my friend," he said, "I thought you were dead."

Before we write off these murderous men as anomalies, consider that we have all been infected by the same energy. Look at the political landscape right now in America. Permanent, unremovable cancellation and demonization coming from the far left. Talk of civil war coming from the far right. Otherism is thriving like a pernicious weed in the land of the free. Do you remember when they referred to America as a "mixing pot"? The stew is not working out so well at the moment, is it?

Travel… real, conscious travel is one tool in changing this direction. Not travel like checking sights off a bucket list. Not travel like staying at the resort, eating buffet, and drinking mai tais every day. No. I'm speaking of travel like this: Going into an unfamiliar territory to meet people who appear different than you, then to discover all your commonalities. A conscious traveler has had this experience. A conscious traveler knows that the other is just a blank canvas onto which is thrown fears and frustrations. A conscious traveler knows that the best way to fairly color this canvas is to connect.

Now, let me tell you another travel story that could have led to the death of our entire planet.

SLIDING INTO THE DRAGON'S LAIR

It was a freezing cold morning in Saint Petersburg when I flipped open my laptop to find an email from an urban explorer. He gave me, under the conditions of anonymity, the coordinates of an abandoned nuclear missile facility near the Estonian border. I rented a car and drove to the spot, eventually arriving at a guard shack with a boom barrier across the small dirt road. A dog started barking in a house about 30 meters away. I expected some security team to come strutting down any minute. No one came. I got out of the car and lifted up the barrier.

Sure enough, beyond a stretch of woods, a little complex opened up. We filmed extensively in a series of fortified buildings and underground bunkers. Nobody was around… Or were they? Someone had left a series of oddities in random rooms. In one there was a noose hanging from the ceiling. In another, scattered mannequins on the concrete floor. A third chamber had an old wooden table in the center with a collection of black and white headshots on it. Was there a serial killer lurking around the complex?

Finally, we found the silos. Tying a rope around a metal railing, I slid down into one. A rusty walkway circled the interior of the massive tube.

There was a 20-meter drop to murky water that filled the bottom of the silo. Who knows how deep that went. I crouched down inside this dragon's lair and soaked it in.

As a child I was deeply disturbed by the end of the cold war. We had get-under-the-table drills in class. I recall the immediate panic when I'd hear emergency sirens blare their warnings as I walked home from school. After a quick calculation, I would deduce that it was the first Tuesday of the month, when they tested the system. The panic subsided, but never completely.

Why did those missiles never launch? What if they had been in the possession of Aum Shinrikyo, the People's Temple, or the men who almost lynched me in Kashmir? The difference between these groups and the governments of the United States and the USSR is clear. One cluster knows how to speak a common language of reason. The other does not. One understands we are all in this together, despite our differences. They know that the loss of common ground could lead to disastrous consequences. Everyone in this camp rationally agrees that it's best not to blow up the world. With the other camp, full of divine mission delusions, there are no such assurances. They have lost the touchstone of reason. They might find it quite glorious to go up in a ball of flame if that would entail the destruction of their enemies.

The only thing that kept us alive through the cold war, I realized as I crouched inside that ICBM silo, was interconnectivity. It's the only thing that will continue to keep us alive, and it's currently being buffeted from all sides.

The best thing I can do, and the best thing you can do, is to hold the fort of reason and empathy. Conscious travel is a valuable tool in breaking down the creeping disease of otherism. When we stay in our bubbles, consuming custom-curated content from our social media apps, or our favorite news channels, the fear and suspicion begin to slither in, like a snake in the garden. When we truly step out of our echo chambers, going into unfamiliar terrain and encountering new people, we break down those divisions.

Back in Moscow, I jumped in a taxi. The driver, as it turned out, had never met an American. I utilized every word of Russian I knew. He dug deep for his English. When all else failed, we shared photos, gestured, and utilized a translator app. There was a certain tilt to our smiles, warmth in our handshake, and understanding in our eyes when we parted ways. We had connected and felt our common humanity. I could imagine him returning to his wife that night, or his friends at the pub, and saying, "I met an American today, and he was actually a really nice guy." These kinds of interactions resonate out to make people second guess their stereotypes. They give us a chance to take a second look at each other with fresh eyes.

A traveler gets the unique opportunity to step out of their society, with all its tensions, and into another, with different divisions. Once you begin to see the absurdity of conflicts abroad, the lessons will eventually lead you to view the ones at home in a new light. For example, when the traveler comes to India and makes a genuine human connection with a dalit (lowest social caste), and then later with someone who is brahmin (highest caste), they will not feel some inherent value difference between them. The brahmin will most likely have more material wealth, but there is no correlation to the character of the person. A dalit is just as likely to be honest, kind, generous, and courageous.

For an Indian, mired in the caste system, this understanding of equality will be harder to see (things have been changing, but the paradigm is not yet dead). However, for a German, Belgian, or Canadian it's easy to recognize the absurdity of classifying someone's value, from birth, due to a caste. The Belgian traveler, witnessing many such harmful divisions during their travels, will soon develop the capability to spot irrational prejudices back at home.

LITTLE CREDIT / LITTLE BLAME

A young kid named Manuel approached me as I was sitting on a rocky shoreline beside a poor Panamanian village. He was curious about my story. When I asked him about his life, he guided me to a little mud-floor hut. Mom was inside baking cinnamon rolls, which she sold for income. As I munched on the delightful pastries, I thought about how different this family's fate would be if the coast near their home had a sandy beach instead of big gray stones. They might be running a little posada, boutique, or coffee-shop. Mom could charge gringos three times the price for the same rolls.

I was born in a country with the world's strongest economy. I have two loving parents. They happened to be middle-class. Somehow, my consciousness moves around in a fairly strong body and inhabits a brain with a decent IQ. I've caught a heap of lucky breaks in my life and avoided many near-death tragedies by a hair's length. Did I choose any of this or do I somehow deserve it? Not any more than Manuel and his mom chose that rocky shoreline.

In his book *The Psychology of Money*, Morgan Housel notes that anything of value in life will require a degree of risk to get it. Nothing that is a worthy goal is a slam dunk. Additionally, nobody is certain how much luck plays into the equation. Of course, it's critical to have contacts, talent, and hard work; but that trinity does not give you a slam dunk.

A few years ago, one of my friends was shopping a sitcom around Hollywood. He had sterling contacts and a very tight script for a pilot episode. A lucky meeting was set up with a top producer who was friends with Adam Sandler. My buddy was nailing the pitch. The producer loved it. Then, unexpectedly, the producer's assistant popped into the room. This guy was new and wanted to prove his value.

My friend finished his presentation. The head honcho was sold. He picked up the phone and said, "I'm calling Adam right now."

Then, the assistant, sitting in the corner and shuffling through the script, suddenly piped up, "Ahhh… I think we should give him one round of notes."

"Yeah?" asked the producer, the phone receiver still in his hand, and the other hand hovering above the dial buttons.

"Yeah. I've got some notes," said the assistant, eager to offer some value.

The producer hung up the phone and sent my friend away with the instruction to get in touch when he was done making the assistant's adjustments. By the time my buddy made the changes, the producer was on a new project which was consuming his time. He moved on. My friend never got another meeting.

What if that assistant had gone for lunch an hour earlier and not made that meeting? What if he'd been with the company longer and didn't feel compelled to add something to the conversation? There is a chance my buddy would be the creator (and perhaps an executive producer) on a network TV show. We'd all be praising his talent and hustle. Now, he gets none of that praise. He did everything right, but his luck ran out at the last minute.

The goofy thing is that we tend to take too much credit for successes and too much blame for failures. Let's look at two fictional people who launch startups:

HEATHER	STACY
Has a solid idea	Has an idea with some flaws
Grinds at work	Works leisurely
Market takes an unfavorable turn due to unpredictable global events	Meets an angel investor at a bar one night

Stacy will be the one giving interviews about her successful idea. It's highly unlikely that she will attribute luck to her good fortune. Heather, sitting on the couch in defeat, would be wise to keep her chin up. Yes, there are undoubtedly things she could have done better, and it's good to learn from those things. However, she was also unlucky.

When we look at where we are in life, and where others are, it's both compassionate and accurate to recognize how most of the factors that brought us to these junctures were totally out of our control:

We did not choose our parents, our brains, or our luck. Let's bring humility and gratitude to the successes and compassion to the bad breaks.

THE MERRY-GO-ROUND OF OTHERS

The things that divide us now are different than they were before. The conscious traveler has seen the traces of history. They've learned about conflicts over divisions that would seem ridiculous to us now.

Consider the thousands of people killed and tortured during the Spanish Inquisition for not adhering to the right kind of Christianity. We wouldn't tolerate the church burning someone at the stake now. It's ludicrous. How about the cold welcome Irish immigrants received in New York City (as most were fleeing the horrible famine on their island). They were treated as sub-human. Businesses would post "Help-Wanted" signs with the caveat that, "Irish need not apply." Cartoons depicted them as ape-like in appearance.

Today, however, any American who can count one shred of Irish DNA (and many who can't) are eager to dress up in green and celebrate their heritage on Saint Patrick's Day. Now, we have different divisions, which one day will seem ridiculous to our descendants, as they celebrate the culture that we once demonized.

ANTI-IMMIGRATION POLITICAL CARTOON DEPICTING AN IRISHMAN
(PUBLISHED 2 SEPTEMBER 1871 IN **HARPER'S WEEKLY**)

With this broad understanding, the traveler sees that humans have a bad habit of perpetually choosing some group to hate. Contemporary thinker Rene Girard believes that when tensions grow in our communities, we look to scapegoat another group for our problems. Conflict resolution specialist Jennifer Jones-Patulli has written that hatred has a seductive appeal for its capability to energize. When a person or group feels disempowered, demonizing another gives the hater a gratifying kind of pep. A negative action plan feels better than no plan at all. It's much easier than wading into the messy work of introspection. A hater's life may continue to be shitty, but at least there is the illusion of doing something about it.

Illusion really is the key word here. If an alien species were to visit, they would probably not parse Jew from Palestinian, Serb from Croatian, or Uyghur from Han. They would, most likely, see us all as earthlings. And, if those aliens were to attack, we might quickly accept that perspective as well. The divisions that we have created for ourselves are what the Hindu mystics would call "maya." Maya is the smoky mirror and the dream glasses that everyone wears. Squirrels, cats, fish, snakes, and tigers probably share something with the invading aliens. They are all impervious to maya. Human beings are the only creatures on this planet that create fictions which both unite and divide us.

GOD, LOST IN A DAYDREAM

Recently, while filming in Kolkata, I tried a radical experiment in perception. This turned out to be a fantastic tool in breaking through otherness and misanthropy. If ever you catch yourself sliding into these negative states, I invite you to try it.

Kolkata, in West Bengal, India, is one of the most densely populated cities in the world. Once you step out of your room, you won't be able to scratch your nuts without someone seeing. There is, literally, a person around every corner. Moving down the public streets, a traveler will experience a clamorous flood of chaotic movement. It is quite easy to feel overwhelmed.

Before I arrived, I had listened to a speech by Alan Watts called *The Mythology of Hinduism*. I won't attempt to recount the ideas with any hope of matching Watt's eloquence (you really must give this one a listen), but I will tell you about the thought experiment it inspired.

For the next couple weeks, I would look at different people on the streets and consider them to be an expression of the divine. When the poor rickshaw bicycle man pedaled by, I would place all my attention on him and think, "There goes God, so deep in the dream of being a poor rickshaw man, that he has forgotten who he really is." In affluent company my thoughts were, "There goes God, so lost in the idea that she's the wealthy heir of this business empire, that she has forgotten who she really is." This experiment will inevitably lead to the mirror at the end of the day. What is the dream in which you are lost?

Let's dig into this idea for a minute. The earth was born out of the universe. Humans were born out of the earth. This seems like an uncontroversial line of solid connection. As clear evidence, we must continually put the earth back into our bodies (in the form of protein, fat, minerals, etc.) or we would quickly wither and physically disappear. In other words, we are compelled to continually re-earth. This should be obvious to us at all times. We should perpetually feel this connection. But, we don't. How could we lose this simple line of reasoning? Why is it so hard to see the world through this lens?

There are devious forces at work. Commercial and political interests tend to push a message of disconnection. It's better to have a consumer, or voter, destabilized so they can be sold on the idea that the right purchase, or vote, will bring some kind of completeness. The subtext of this message, blasted at us all the time, is that you are like a bird perched on the branch of a tree. A bird without a nest. If you buy these things, and re-elect Senator Trustme into office, the nest will finally form underneath you.

Are you a bird on a tree? Where did you come from little birdie? Did we not come *from* the tree? Therefore, are we not the leaves of that tree? Could we say that the leaves, just as the branches and roots, are both part of the tree *and* the tree itself. The leaves, however, being the conscious part of this special Tree of Life, can dream. They can fall into the collective dream, or maya, of the culture. A dream about birds struggling to find elusive nests.

Even if you find these musings to be complete poppycock, simply experimenting with this idea completely changes the mental landscape. The importance of such a perspective isn't how close it is to absolute truth (if we could ever determine such a thing), but rather how it empowers us to become better humans.

Inside the sarcophagus chamber of the pyramid of Unis is one of the first depictions of the Ouroboros. The symbol can also be found in ancient Nordic and Greek culture. What are our ancestors trying to tell us with this image of a snake eating its own tail? That life is cyclical, and, importantly, one thing. The reptile is errantly eating itself because the head has become unidentified with the tail. The head is under the illusion that the tail belongs to the other. From a distance we can say, "Silly snake. There is no other." Yet, you, the traveler, might begin to recognize yourself as this reptile, walking through the world and continually dividing it into two things: Lonely old me and everything else.

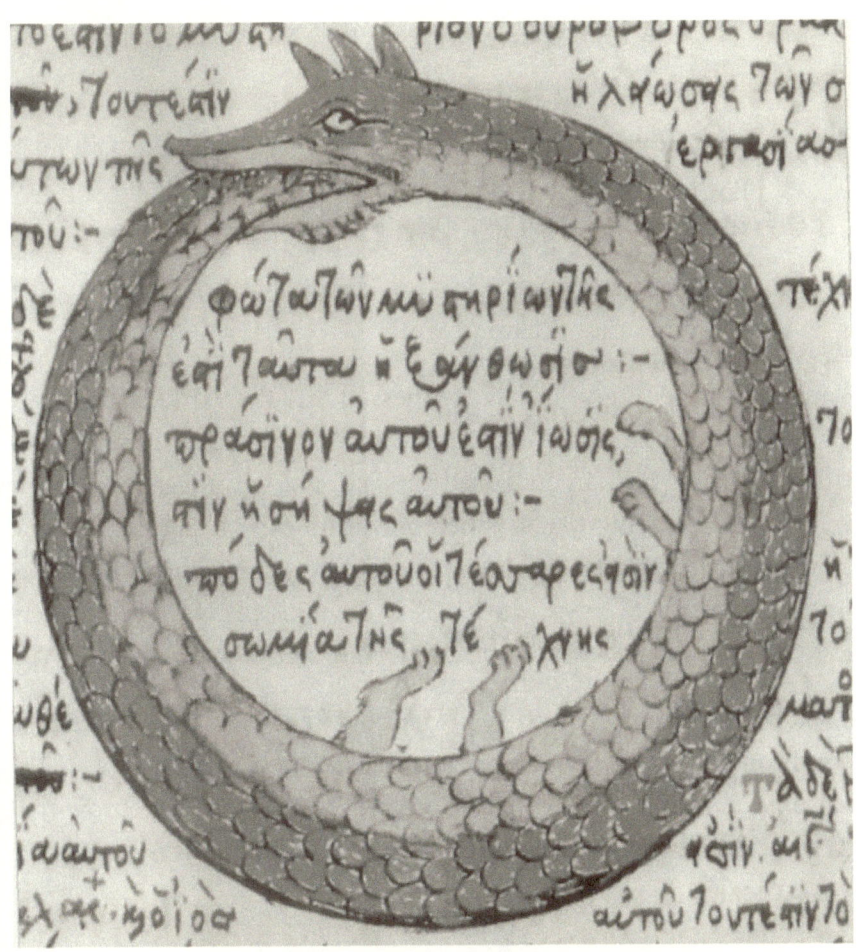

1478 DRAWING BY THEODOROS PELECANOS OF AN ALCHEMICAL
TRACT ATTRIBUTED TO SYNESIUS

Ponder this:

- Is there a particular group of people that get under your skin? Can you think of a way to increase your compassion and understanding for them? In what ways do you have things in common?

- If you were to list some of the great things that have happened for you, how many of them involved a degree of luck? How about your great disappointments?

- If you were lost in some kind of dream right now, how would you describe that dream of you?

You, the watchful traveler, have witnessed that the world is full of divisions that extend into your own life and heart. You understand that these divisions are largely based on fictional narratives. You know that xenophobia, bigotry, and demonization can be smashed by real travel. It doesn't matter if the journey is to the other side of the world, or the other side of town. The key is to meet people who seem different than you, and then to discover all your commonalities.

You, the perceptive traveler, also know that the only functional common language we have as a species, which could move us towards well-being and away from suffering, is reason. You know that to understand someone is to see their shared humanity.

WHEN THINGS GO AWRY, THE TRUE ADVENTURE BEGINS.

The best experiences can't be forced and they come when you least expect it. You don't find misadventure, it finds you.

~ S.A. Tawks

*M*y travel buddy, James, had a habit of overpacking. His heavy luggage was perpetually an issue for him, and, since we were traveling together, it became my problem as well. On a trip to Turkey, my frustrations boiled over in the capital city of Ankara. His backpack, straining under the weight of many unnecessary items (including a hair dryer), gave up the ghost on a hot day as we were walking into town. One of the shoulder straps ripped right off the bag as we trudged from the bus station towards our hotel.

"I can't go on," he announced. The bag was too heavy to carry the rest of the walk with one strap. We had to find a place right there and then to fix it. This was a problem for me. I had an itinerary, for the love of god! It was critical that we get to the hotel quickly so that we could visit the Museum of Anatolian Civilizations before it closed.

We hurriedly asked around for someone nearby who could fix the bag and got directed down a hill into a decidedly local neighborhood. There was a tailor, but the door was locked. The neighbor suggested we leave the bag with him. He would ask the tailor to fix it when the man returned.

"How long will that take?" I inquired.

"Two to three hours," he replied.

I threw my hands up in a dramatic display of frustration. This was the worst!

The neighbor suggested we kill time in a local tea house, a staple in many Islamic cultures. These are places where Muslim men can enjoy the few vices allowed to them: drinking caffeine, smoking cigarettes, and playing backgammon. Women are strongly encouraged to stay away.

We pushed open the glass door and entered the smokey room full of idle chatter and the clack-clack of backgammon chips moving around wooden boards. Scanning the place for an empty seat, I caught the gaze of a couple of men in the middle of the joint. They beckoned us to come and gestured at the backgammon board in front of them.

Call it beginner's luck. Somehow, I beat the local man who waved us over. He was furious. Really. As I was putting him in the ditch, towards the end of our match, word must have traveled out of the cafe. Perhaps, a couple of children were dispatched as messengers. Just moments after the game was over, as I took a satisfied sip from a tiny teacup, basking in the victory, a hush fell over the room. The front doors swung open. In walked the backgammon king.

The man was a local legend. The neighborhood's favorite son. He was charismatic, handsome, successful, and the best backgammon player that side of the Bosphorus.

As we sat down to play, the cafe filled with spectators. Kids pressed their faces against the window to get a glimpse of our contest. I picked up the dice and rolled.

Things were going remarkably well. I had a hot hand. Too hot. Doubles kept tumbling out of my palm. My chips were speeding across the board, concerningly faster than his. The oxygen in the room seemed to be diminishing. Things got quiet and tense. I began to ponder the wisdom of winning this game but had some trouble considering how to throw it. Was it really ethical to intentionally lose? How could I throw the game and not make it obvious? No... the right thing was to play my best. Let fate decide who to adorn as the victor.

The backgammon king made a late comeback. He may have cheated. Doesn't matter. What does matter is, when his last chips came off the board, just barely ahead of mine, there was a giant exhale in the cafe. Then, it erupted in cheerful banter, backslapping, and laughter. My friend and I were embraced. It was just another hum-drum day at the cafe until the two Americans came through the door and stirred shit up. We had provided everyone a good dose of drama with a happy ending. Whatever frustrations I had walking into the joint were long gone. This was the spot to be.

We never got to that thing on my itinerary. If that backpack hadn't broken, and we had walked through those museums, gazing at the exhibits, would I remember any of them now, over two decades later? Probably not. The backgammon battle in the cafe was the highlight of the whole trip. I made a genuine connection with real, salt-of-the-earth Turks. We shared a roller coaster ride of drama, tension, and levity. Since that day, this has been a great observation of my travels: misadventure trumps straight adventure every day. Now, when something goes awry, I say, "Fuck!" Then, in a few minutes, it occurs to me that the game is on. It's time to get excited.

When our film crew got stranded in the Singapore airport, because we didn't have the right visas for our connecting flight to Vietnam, the game was afoot. We got a whole Malaysian episode out of that mistake, then went to Vietnam. When a nail went through my motorcycle's rear tire, beside "the Wall" separating the U.S. and Mexico, a new adventure began. A friendly lady from a nearby trailer park drove me around the small town looking for a solution. I got to know her and a bunch of other locals.

Sometimes the call to misadventure can appear quite troubling. Maybe you've missed an expensive flight. Perhaps your wallet was stolen. Maybe, as it happened to me once, you've been unexpectedly dropped in the middle of the Caucasus mountains with scant daylight remaining and many miles to any kind of shelter. In such situations, one must slide into a process.

> **Stay calm** - Every list like this starts with "stay calm." I used to think this was unnecessary to mention, but experience has taught that the reminder is helpful. Panic is a bitch. Panic will lead to irrational decisions. If you're in a real bind, irrational decisions dig you in deeper. If you are in a life-threatening situation, irrational decisions will kill you. The minute something really goes off the rails, take a breath. If you have time, take a moment. Perhaps, sit down for a cup of tea and a good think. Everything will go smoother for this step.

> **Look for the next best step** - Let go of all the stuff you've lost control over. Don't waste time considering long-term implications. You can deal with that in the future. Things will pan out. Don't get into the woulda-shoulda trap of berating yourself or

your travel buddy. It's done. It is what it is. Simply figure out "what is the best thing to do now?" Then, "what is the next thing to do?" Focus on the most important steps one at a time. If you are in danger, get out of it. If you need food, water, or shelter; secure it. Once you're not going to die, you can exhale. At some point in this process, things will begin to feel light enough to embrace the situation.

- **Have fun with it** - Now that you are not going to die, run out of water/food, or sleep in the gutter; things really don't have to be that bleak anymore. Consider that every possession you own will at some point get lost, break, or be stolen. Money comes and goes. We are all going to get old and die. It's a tragedy **and** it's a comedy. If we can't laugh about this stuff, the existential dread would be too much to bear. Furthermore, what fun is a movie in which everything goes according to plan? A good story requires drama, and drama requires some tension. As we sit on our rocking chairs, winding down from a life well-lived, we will recall these kinds of moments with a grin.

- **Ask some people for assistance** - This is one of the real treats of misadventure. I'm forced to humble myself and ask for support. What I rediscover, over and over, is that most people are good and are eager to help. As great as it feels to be saved, it feels even better to save someone. I once found a missing hiker on a mountain. She was rattled and embarrassed by the predicament. I was on cloud nine. It felt so damn good to come to the rescue. Misadventure almost always loops other people into resolving your situation. If you are grateful, they will feel satisfied to be of service. Everyone walks away from the situation with more faith in the goodness of humanity.

❯ **Tell the story** - There is no story better than a misadventure story. And there is no better way for you to remember the joys of that misadventure, and prepare yourself for the next, than to recount your tale to others. Share that gem with fellow travelers, family, and friends. Learn how to control your pace, volume, and tone to maximize the enjoyment for the listener. Pause at the right moments and hold the tension. Remove unnecessary details, backstories, and tangential points that don't serve the central narrative. A honed travel story is a wonderful thing to have in your pocket for any social gathering.

THE FRIENDLY HELPER COMES IN UNEXPECTED FORM

When the throng of people began running past me, I could see the fear on their faces.

"Silly superstitions," I mumbled to myself, "They must think the gods are angry." I stood my ground.

Then, I saw the barrage of bricks flying through the air. Suddenly, a small hand wrapped around mine. I looked down to see a child no older than 7. "Come with me," he said.

It was the late 90s. I had come to a small city in Nepal to witness a hazardous festival. A large chariot was pulled through narrow city streets, smashing patios and roofs along its journey. Giant ropes stretched out from the contraption, which were pulled by hundreds of Hindu pilgrims. Sitting on top of the vehicle, which resembled a three-story temple, were priests. They attempted to shout directions down to the masses that yanked them along. With all the noise and commotion, it took a minute for someone on the ropes to hear. Then, it took a couple of minutes more for the command to spread down the line. Imagine, in your city, a driving school where the teacher's words are delayed by 30 seconds.

I tried to follow as closely as I could. At one point, the chariot smashed the corner of a building and debris fell around me. I dove to the side and was helped back to my feet by a few locals. Undeterred, I continued to follow the chariot as it arrived at a large square. There was no indication that mayhem was about to erupt.

In the center of the plaza, the two sides of town began to engage in a tug of war with the wheeled temple in the center. The python thick ropes groaned with the force. The chariot creaked like a pirate ship on the high seas. The battle was fierce. Then, something unexpected happened. One of the gigantic wooden wheels popped off the axle. The chariot leaned over hard, barely avoiding a full collapse onto its side (which no doubt would have decimated some of the priests riding on top). There was a long, pregnant pause in the action. Then, people started to run.

Generally speaking, when a mob runs past you with fear in their eyes, it's a solid choice to run with them. You can figure out the reasons later. What inspired me to stay still, feet planted, was not some kind of fear paralysis. It was a mix of hubris and ignorance. I assumed the panicked mob, running past me, was under the belief that the gods must be angry about the collapsed chariot. I didn't fear these gods[8]!

---

[8] See Realization 1 on deadly mermen. Classic example.

The movement of things flying through the air caught my attention. Bricks, with heavy thuds, now began to rain around me. This is when the child grabbed my hand and led me quickly away. We snaked through narrow alleys and up steep staircases, eventually arriving at a perch with a view of the square below.

Unable to resolve their heated competition by tug of war, the two sides of town had begun to rip the bricks out of the plaza and hurl them at each other. I guess they had some grudges. The priests, immobilized and disempowered on their broken contraption, futilely blew large horns in an attempt to bring calm to the dueling mobs. A guy, leaving the melee, walked past me, a blood-soaked towel on his head. That would have been me, if not for this kid.

The conscious traveler has met the friendly helper in their journeys. Just like the dwarves and toads in fairy tales, they don't always seem appealing. I could have easily dismissed that child in Nepal, to my peril, as being too young to know what was what. Likewise, other helpers have appeared in the form of street touts and hoodlums. It's quite often the person you're most inclined to ignore who has the most important message. When things go sideways, as they did for me in that plaza, they are often the one who will save you.

WOLVES IN SHEEP'S CLOTHING

There is a fine line to walk in identifying the helper. A dangerous character, who poses as a helper, roams the landscape. He is a wolf in sheep's clothing. Wherever naive tourists amble, scammers swim like sharks. Their delivery, practiced over countless repetitions, is as smooth as Irish butter. I recently watched with fascination as a man who saluted me on the streets of Pisa transitioned from greeting, to gift giving, to a request for money. Although I was aware of what was happening, his performance was so enthralling that euros came out of my pocket as if it were their destiny. But a cheap bracelet sale is one thing. The spell of the scammer can drag a traveler into the deep end. The deep end is where you can lose hundreds if not thousands. The deep end is where you are in physical danger.

Gavin de Becker, in his excellent book *The Gift of Fear*, describes the behaviors of a con-artist. Here are some, from his list, that I've seen in my travels:

- **Forced teaming** - When a stranger quickly drops the pronoun "we" and begins to refer to you both as some unit or team, it should raise the alarms.

- **Typecasting** - A scammer in Thailand once challenged my manhood as a tactic. He teased me for not being brave enough to get on his boat. I want to be viewed as a courageous man. He was hoping I would do as he wished to prove myself. It had nothing to do with courage, however. He was charging 10x the normal rate for such a ride.

- **Charm** - The key here is to distinguish between someone who is simply charismatic, and someone who is laying on the charm. I ask myself, "Why are they buttering me up?" and, "If they want something. What is it?"

- **Loan sharking** - A scammer will often do you a favor up front in order to put you in their debt. I had a stranger once buy me a cup of coffee. Later, he asked me to get in his car and help him pick something up from a friend's place. I tested his intentions with a subversion technique I'll share below. His responses made me feel unsafe to get in the vehicle.

❯ **Refusing a "No"** - It's important to respect your decision to say "no." If that word comes out of your mouth, or sounds in your head, honor the impulse. De Becker writes, "If you let someone talk you out of the word 'no,' you might as well wear a sign that reads, 'You are in charge.'" In Belgrade a pretty girl flirted with me in front of the national theater. It seemed too easy. There was an awkwardness to her body language. Then suddenly her male friend appeared, with odd timing, and suggested we all go to a party. I dropped a polite "no." They pushed. I doubled down with a stronger "no."

When I'm in doubt of a stranger's intentions, I test them by subverting their plan and watching their reaction carefully. A scammer often has a well-practiced routine that includes trusted colleagues and exact locations. Take them off this track and suddenly they are improvising. The shift from practiced to unpracticed is often noticeable.

TUK-TUK?

As I walked towards Wak Saket temple, I noticed a businessman was going in my direction. Occasionally, I would get ahead of him on the sidewalk and, sometimes, he would be ahead of me. It was a crowded walkway. At one point, we found ourselves side by side.

"Nice day," he said to me casually.

"Going to work?" I asked, noting his suit and briefcase.

"Yeah," he replied, "where are you going?"

"I'm headed to the temple," I said.

The man slowed down as a look of concern came over his face. "Oh… the temples are closed. It's a Buddhist holiday."

"Oh… I didn't know that." My shoulders slumped. Bummer.

The man looked at his watch briefly, like he was in a hurry to get somewhere.

"I'll tell you what, do you have a map of some kind?"

Yes! I had one stuffed in the guidebook that was swinging in my hand.

He pointed out a few temples and sights, fairly far from our location, that would be open on that day. What a nice guy!

"You could take a bus to get there, or you could take a tuk-tuk. Wait, what day is today?" he asked.

"It's Friday," I said.

"Right, Friday!" He clapped his hands enthusiastically. "Tuk-Tuks are half price on Friday. That's lucky. Oh… here is one now."

As the three wheeled vehicle pulled up, a doubt sprouted in my head. It was the expression of the driver, like he was expecting this moment. I wasn't sure of anything funny yet, and I didn't want to offend this businessman if he was being genuinely helpful. So, I decided to subvert the plan and see what happened.

"You know, I've taken a lot of tuk-tuks in Bangkok, but I haven't experienced a bus ride yet," I declared, "so I'll take the bus." I paid very close attention to his reaction… and I saw it.

The businessman's face fell into a frown. I took him off script and he didn't like it. "Why would you take the bus?" he said.

"It's a new experience for me. I love having new experiences. That's what travel is all about, right?"

"Just take the tuk-tuk. It's right here." Frustration colored his face.

It was now obvious. Why would a rushed executive be so invested in my transportation choices? I walked off and glanced back to see the two men conferring. They were undoubtedly discussing what went wrong, and how they'd fix it. The scam would be tighter when the next traveler fell into their sights.

A conscious traveler is cautious when a stranger approaches them. Awareness should always heighten if this stranger wants to change their plan and lead them to another location. In the company of a stranger, never become physically isolated from escape or help. When in doubt, subvert the plan into a direction of more safety and backup. So, for example, if the stranger invites you to a drink at a special bar he knows, a good response is to accept the drink, but in the bar you know. Don't go to his bar for the second round until you've verified from a trusted source that it's legit.

The secret is not to become so fearful of strangers that amazing connections are lost. For every scammer, there are three friendly locals. The trick is to separate the sheep from the wolves.

While filming a food show in Cuba, a man on the street approached the team. He wanted to sell us some cigars but was also curious about our story. He asked where we had filmed. I listed off some restaurants. He informed me that I was covering the food scene for rich locals, as most folks did not have a budget to eat out. If I wanted to show the real food scene in Havana, I'd have to film in a home. He offered to guide us, on the spot, to the apartment of some friends. Maybe they'd be having dinner soon. I was leery of following this man somewhere but decided to proceed with heightened attention.

The entrance to the apartment block was pitch black. I told the crew to stay behind as I walked in. On the other side of the passage dim light bulbs illuminated the center courtyard of a shanty complex. There were many elderly and children about. I waved the crew in. There, we filmed a wonderful little piece with a small family living in relative poverty. We provided some refreshments and I paid them a tiny sum of money for their time. Everyone came out smiling. None of this would have happened without a friendly helper on the street. I had to proceed cautiously, however, to ensure he was not a wolf.

AVALANCHE LADY

One key to securing the friendly helper is to extend the conversation. Be curious about the people who cross your traveler's path. Think of the possibility that they might be there for a reason. They may have something to teach you or to show you.

Walking down the streets of Bolzano, Italy with my cameraman, a sliding door opened beside us and the most delicious aromas came wafting out.

"You hungry?" I asked him.

"Let's do it," he replied.

Inside was a kind of cafeteria system where one slides a tray along the track, asking for food at different stations. With loaded plates, we arrived at the cashier.

"Carta dello studente," said the signora at the register.

"Can I just pay cash?" I asked.

"You need student card," she replied. Apparently, this was part of a university.

"Credit card," I countered, pulling out everything I had in my wallet.

The lady shook her head. A small moment of exasperation bloomed. Were we going to have to return these trays?

"I got it," said a woman who had come behind us in line. "I'll pay with my student card and you can give me cash."

Whew! She saved the day. We paid her back and thanked her. Our interaction could have ended right there, but I suggested we sit together. She was alone after all, and, in my philosophy, it's always better to share a meal with good company. Deciding to extend this interaction with a stranger turned into a huge boon. She was a friendly helper.

The woman was doing research on avalanche rescue techniques. I asked if she knew any of the helicopter rescue teams who cover the Italian Dolomites. She knew them well. Within a few days we were on one of those helicopters filming a drill. It was a thrilling experience to be lifted up on a cable into the chopper, and excellent content for our show.

On your travels, use discernment to spot the scammers, and awareness to identify the friendly helpers. You are the hero of your journey, and every hero has antagonists who test their resolve and wits. The hero also needs to recognize the accomplices who act as guides through the maze of life.

MAGIC TALISMANS AND SUPERPOWERS

The hero usually wields some kind of tool which is crucial to success in their journey. Perseus had a cap of invisibility, Achilles wore impenetrable armor, and King Arthur carried a famous sword. The traveler also has a quiver they can draw from when trouble comes hither.

- **Stoicism** - If you think your travels have their ups and downs, have a look at the life of Roman Emperor Marcus Aurelius. He ruled in a time of continual military confrontations and a wave of bubonic plague, which doomed his brother to a horrific death. Yet, when you read his private journal, he appears to be the most even-keeled guy on the planet. Marcus had a world view heavily influenced by the philosophy of stoicism, which was popular amongst the Romans and Greeks. Let's look at a few of the philosophy's practices and see how they can benefit us as travelers.

▸ **Problem reframing** - The stoics encouraged turning every challenge on its head. If it's preventing you from doing X, then it must be allowing you to do Y. As I was leaving Palenque, in the south of Mexico, my bus got pulled over at a random traffic stop. I got singled out as the only gringo. They wanted to see my paperwork. It became quickly apparent that the little immigration stub, that was important to hold onto, had been lost. On top of that, the official who stamped my passport at the airport must have been out of ink. In a nutshell, there was no evidence that I had entered the country legally. After a short imprisonment in a police van, I was instructed to go to the city of Villahermosa and drop myself into the jaws of the slow grinding bureaucracy of immigration services. This was certainly problematic, as I was now queued in the system behind hundreds of refugees from Central and South America. However, I came to Mexico with the objective of having authentic and memorable experiences. I was also interested in the life of these immigrants. I was getting all that in a town with zero tourists. Eventually, I had to call a lawyer in Mexico City and drop some money. Now I have a lawyer in Mexico. A year later, I was relaxing in his rooftop pool in Puerto Escondido.

▸ **Premeditatio malorum** - We tend to give a lot of weight to the bad things that happen, and less to the good. Twenty people might be super nice to you on your first day in Barcelona, but it's the one guy who is an asshole who you will remember. Think of all the miles you've traveled on sketchy transportation (bald tires, overloaded axles, underslept drivers). Usually, you arrive with no issue. Yet, that one blown tire that leaves you on the side of the road for hours can seem like a curse from the gods.

The stoics had a technique for flipping this script. They would take a moment to consider all the terrible things that could have happened but didn't. Imagine if one of the thousands of mosquitos that bit you in Oaxaca had dengue. Happens to people all the time. Imagine if that bus you took through the Himalayas in the rainstorm had rolled just one tire off the edge of the road. Imagine that this morning, when you bent over like a crane and lifted your heavy backpack off the ground, your back went out. Every day that disaster doesn't strike is indeed a day to celebrate. This exercise helps us appreciate our fortune.

▶ **The spectrum of control** - You can quickly parse any situation into one of three buckets: Things of which we have total control, limited control, and zero control. Straight off the top, whatever we can't control (the weather being an obvious example) should be completely embraced. What good does it do to waste even a minute of life bitching about the rain? What could be gained from such complaints, other than a plunge into a negative victim state? The clouds are not listening.

We have partial control about how our traveling buddies might react to this rain. If we complain, it will sour their experience of the moment. If we pivot to a positive plan, we help them frame it positively as well. This pivot is where we have total control. The rain falling is out of our hands, but the story we tell ourselves about the situation is our story to narrate. The faster you can let go of the plan to sunbathe, and get enthusiastic about a rainy-day plan, the quicker your psychological relief. Maybe tuck into that cute cafe and read the book that's been on your list forever. Maybe take a hike and enjoy the diminished crowds, the pitter patter of the rain on the canopy, and the tiny streams forming through the landscape.

The stoics believed we must embrace our fate (amor fati) and not try to push it away. Life gives us a series of stages to act on. Until the curtain call, we have no choice but to play our role. The only variable is: How good is the performance and how happy or miserable is the actor?

Author Tara Brach, in her classic book *Radical Acceptance*, has a useful exercise in this vein. She invites the reader to consider everything about their current experience. For me, at this very moment, I'm sitting in front of a laptop in Bangkok. I'm typing this out with no idea if it's going to be well received by the reader. My arm itches from a mosquito bite. I'm a bit hungry as lunchtime approaches. I've finished filming an episode of *Road Less Traveled* in Thailand and am a bit unsure we have enough content in the bag. I'm aware that my savings and investments are much lower than they were three months ago. There is war in Ukraine. I haven't seen most of my good friends in months. My right arm won't extend fully due to an injury. There is a Dua Lipa song playing in the distance.

Take a beat and run this list for yourself. What's happening right now around you and in you? On Tara's advice, as you think about each particular thing, say, "No!" in your head. For example, I might think, "No. I wish that mosquito hadn't bitten me. No. I don't like that song playing in the distance. I wish they'd change it." As you reject every aspect of your current reality, pay attention to how your state begins to change. When you feel crappy enough, stop.

Now, go through the list again and say, "Yes" to everything in your awareness. Notice the immediate difference? Thanks to Tara, whenever I find myself anxious and tense, I do a quick scan of my situation. Is there something I'm saying "no" to? Can I change it, and, if not, how can I embrace it?

The right pack - When things go awry, what you've got in your pockets and on your back suddenly becomes a lot more important. If you get stranded in a rural area, it would be really handy to have some cash. Credit cards begin to lose their power as you travel outwards from wealthy urban centers. If you get stranded in the wilderness, it would be super-duper to have some water on you. The second you become dehydrated, your decisions get worse. Nobody plans for these things to happen, but they will.

Whenever I step out of my lodging for a day of adventure, I always have a small day-pack slung over my shoulders. Between that and my pockets, here is what I'm carrying:

- 1-3 liters of water (in a bladder or steel bottle. Free to refill at fountains and restaurants. Saves on single-use plastic pollution).

- Warmer layer (usually a puffy jacket). Even if you are vacationing in the hottest ring of hell, carry another layer. In Venezuela, I got onto a "deluxe" bus for a six-hour journey. I was wearing a sweaty t-shirt. I had one other sweaty t-shirt in my bag. The bus quickly became as cold as Berlin in winter. I walked up to the driver, encased in a plexiglass cubicle, and complained. He looked at me like I was crazy. I turned to face all the passengers and tried to gather support. "Hace frío, no?" They looked at me like I was crazy. Then, I noticed they all had coats and blankets. Apparently, this was a thing in the steamy tropical climate: Get on a super cold bus and snuggle up for a change. As I suffered through that ride this policy was cemented. Always carry a warmer layer.

- Phone charging cord.

- Headlamp (You might get caught out in the dark. Sometimes there is a tunnel, shadowy ruins, or a cave to explore).

- A bamboo cutlery set.

- Sunscreen.

- Cash (stashed in a few locations).

- Copy of my passport (now on the phone).

- Map of the area (On the phone. Don't rely on signal. Download it onto your device. Maps.me is a good option).

If I'm going into the wilderness for a hike, I'll also carry:

▶ Lighter (To start a fire if I get stranded and it gets dark).

▶ Teacup candle (incredibly helpful for starting a fire).

▶ Knife.

▶ First aid kit.

▶ External battery (to charge phone and headlamp if needed).

When a misadventure occurs, you will pat yourself on the back for having the right gear. It doesn't count if it's back in your room. There is nothing like pulling a warm puffy out of your bag when the conditions get unexpectedly cold or having those extra bills to buy your way out of a jam.

❯ Fitness - Once, in Bogota, Colombia, I was in a foot race with seven thugs. They either wanted my money, to beat me up, or both. I'm not sure. It started with them surrounding me on the street. They thought I was unaware of their encirclement. I broke into a full sprint. At one point, the closest guy was just a few meters away. Two blocks later, I had a 20-meter lead on the group. They were gassing. I hit a busy intersection and was able to cross a gap in the traffic. By the time they arrived, a slew of fast-moving vehicles divided us. I jumped into a taxi and fled the scene. Fortunately, I was in better shape than these fellas. What if I had not been?

In 1902, a Frenchman named Georges Herbert, was on a navy ship near the coast of Martinique when a violent volcanic eruption occurred. He jumped off his ship, which was leaving, and onto another boat headed back to the island. Georges is credited for helping around 700 people escape the disaster. At times he climbed up the sides of buildings and lifted heavy rubble off the injured. The experience formed a lifelong philosophy in Georges: "Être fort pour être utile." Be strong and be useful. He developed a fitness paradigm called the natural method, which is seen as a predecessor to parkour.

Of course, we all have our physical limitations. I will never be as strong as The Rock or as fast as Usain Bolt. I can let go of those standards. However, I don't want to ever think, "I *could* have outrun that thief if I was in decent shape." Or, worse, "I *could* have swum out into that lake and saved that kid…"

There is a reason James Bond, Wonder Woman, and Batman are in peak shape. They have to be. They are misadventure specialists. When it comes calling for you, or someone around you, the more conditioned you are for strength, speed, and endurance, the higher the odds for a happy ending.

> **Journaling** - A misadventure happens for a brief moment. How you remember that experience will stay with you for a long time. It's hugely beneficial in your travels, and life, to digest the day in writing. Putting things down on paper helps you look at them from different angles and extract the good. What did you learn? What would you do differently in a similar situation? What could have been better or worse?

Studies have shown journaling to reduce anxiety, improve sleep, increase confidence, boost memory, and refine communication skills. A who's who of famous people have considered this an essential practice. Add your name to that list.

Personally speaking, journaling helps me sort through any stressful events and reframe them. I reiterate what my values are so they stay top of mind. I write down important to-do items so I can mentally set them down for a while. Once they are on paper, I don't have to juggle them in my mind. I write to myself in the tone of a best friend/life-coach. Always supportive and encouraging.

- **Gratitude** - This might seem cheesy, but the science is solid. Gratitude moves you into positive emotion, extracts more juice from good experiences, improves health, strengthens your ability to deal with adversity, and enhances your relationships.

  - List a few in your journal on every entry. There must have been some specific moment during the day that is worth recalling. How about that tasty croissant at the bakery? Remember how the sun popped out of the clouds just as you got to the hilltop? What about that local who was extra friendly with you… They didn't have to do that, but they did.

  - Go out of your way to say, "Thank you" and drop compliments. When you notice someone doing something cool or admirable, point it out. Everyone likes to be seen. If your hotel room is sparkling clean, leave a little change and a note for the maid. If someone gives you good service, hook them up with a tip and tell them what you liked.

▶ Be personally grateful, at the end of the day, for all the ways you treated yourself well or lived up to your values. You took a walk to get 10,000 steps because you care about your health. You kept your cool in a stressful situation and de-escalated a conflict. You told the truth when it wasn't easy to do so. Good job! Pat yourself on the back for all the ways you stepped up. Tell yourself you'll do better next time in all the ways you faltered.

With these tools in hand, the misadventures of travel will easily transition to a treasure chest of good stories. Eventually, you'll get a gleam in your eye as soon as trouble begins. The game is afoot!

Ponder this:

❯ Have you experienced some serious misadventure in your travels? How did you get through it? Have you turned that experience into a well-honed story?

❯ Have you met friendly helpers and scammers during your travels? How do you parse the two?

❯ Do you currently utilize any of the 'magic powers and talismans' listed above? Did that list inspire you to incorporate more for the next trip? Which ones?

You, the resilient traveler, know that when things go awry, the door to misadventure has cracked open. You can either suffer, holding on to what is gone, or walk through that door to something quite memorable. You also know that there are two kinds of characters who will be waiting on the other side: scammers and helpers. You have developed the skills to evade the tricks of the former while opening up to the magical assistance of the latter. You, the wise traveler, are physically ready for trouble, and have all the gear needed to cruise through jams. You are mentally prepared for difficulty with the right techniques and practices that turn all of the road's bumps into empowering memories.

AHA! 5

YOU CAN'T SAVE EVERYONE

. . . .

The purpose of life is not to be happy. It is to be useful, to be honorable, to be compassionate, to have it make some difference that you have lived and lived well.

~ Ralph Waldo Emerson

I hopped into a shared tuk-tuk on the dusty, pot-holed streets of Imphal, the capital city of Manipur. I had met some great people in town, but frankly, I was eager to leave. The city was on the bottom end of the charm spectrum. There were almost no parks, fountains, plazas, or art for the people to enjoy. It was just barely functional. Poorly designed structures for houses and business, streets choked with horn blaring traffic, and terrible air quality. I had the luxury of leaving, but most citizens of Imphal do not have the same plate of options. This included the kid who was sitting in the tuk-tuk I jumped into. He turned to me and started a conversation.

During the five-minute ride, I learned that he had been on the way to a job at a car wash. It began to rain just as he arrived, so he was sent back home at his own expense. He lost money that day through no fault of his own. He was a smart, articulate young man. He said that he was desperate to make a friend in America. He believed that a more fulfilling life was attainable, if someone would just throw him a rope. His soft brown eyes locked onto mine with a silent, but powerful plea. Would I be that savior?

"No," I decided quickly, though my heart went out to the kid. In my travels, I have met thousands of people in this young man's position. It would literally be impossible to save every one of them. In a parallel universe, where I lived in Imphal for the summer, the kid and I struck up a friendship, and I came to the conviction that he would do great things with the right support... Yes, I might dedicate the time and resources to helping him. In this universe, where we shared a brief interaction, I looked him in the eye, listened, passed on words of encouragement, and got out of the tuk-tuk at my destination.

You will struggle with this. You will probably struggle with my reasoning on this. It came to me with much struggle. One day, if it hasn't happened already, you will venture into a destination that has a much poorer economy than your own. Hands will be outstretched. Desperate looking people will plead for your financial assistance. Your desire to help will collide with the deep understanding that you can never fill that empty well. It will rattle your soul. I wrestled with some kind of personal policy for decades. Now, I finally have a blueprint, and I am at peace with it.

Inspired by a question posed in the book *Wanting*, by Luke Burgis, I decided to rank my values in a journal. The idea is that, one day, a couple of your values might come into conflict, and it's best to know ahead of time what the pecking order is. For an extreme example, perhaps you have 'honesty' as a top value. You vow to never tell a lie. You also have 'protect people from unnecessary suffering' on that jumbled list. You just so happen to live in Poland in the 1940s and the SS is at your door asking if you have seen any Jews. They are right under your feet in the basement. Which value trumps the other? Are you going to be honest?

Now, let's bring those values to money. What is the list of priorities for the value you want your wealth to create? Lynne Twist, in her book *The Soul of Money*, speaks of having one's finances flowing like a river towards the things that resonate to your heart.

❯ Who are the artists you'd like to support because their creations hold intrinsic, critical value?

❯ What are your passions and how can you financially support them?

❯ Where could you alleviate the most amount of suffering in the world, in the most effective manner?

Once you have these answers dialed in, it's clear that any money which flows in a different direction must suck from these primary dedications. Going back to the river analogy; every time a canal gets dug which diverts water out, less water is going downstream. You get enough canals pulling water out, you've got something looking like the Colorado River entering Mexico. In order to accomplish what is most dear to your heart, finances and time must be doled out in a prioritized manner. There are many reasons why the panhandler might not be a good choice for these finite resources:

❯ In some metropolises, beggars are recruited by a mafia, who collect the lion's share of the money. If business is going well, these sleazeballs will yank more kids from nearby villages to hold out their hands. In other words, your money could have a direct connection to pulling a kid out of a rural laborer life, in exchange for an urban beggar life. Exactly the opposite of your intentions.

❯ A person at rock bottom is often not helped by a carte blanche budget. They may not know how to effectively alleviate their suffering. Perhaps, their unskillfulness with finances is, at least partially, what has them in the difficult spot. A reputable charity will probably be more efficient in turning your cash into the most effective kind of help. Or, if you'd like to take that effort on your shoulders, perhaps you could allocate money in a way that seems best. Rather than handing out straight cash, buy someone a meal, a course in Javascript programming, or a clean set of clothes for a job interview.

❯ A panhandler (speaking strictly of someone who is not offering anything in exchange for money) could have their victimhood affirmed with every dollar they obtain. Furthermore, they suffer the opportunity cost of not pursuing a more fruitful line of effort. On the other hand, the struggling artist, vendor, or shoe shiner will have their work ethic eroded by every dollar, rupee, or peso which the panhandler earns above them. The money, meant to help, becomes a tool of disempowerment.

MARIO'S EMPANADAS

Imagine Mario sets up a little empanada stand on the street. He and his wife spend a good part of the morning preparing the food. Just as they open for business, a beggar posts up beside them. Over the course of the day, more people put change into that beggar's hand than into Mario's business. This goes on for weeks. At what point is Mario going to say, "Fuck the empanadas, I'm just going to shake a cup." Each coin a passerby hands the beggar tempts Mario closer to that decision. That would be a shame. If Mario folds his business, he might make more money the next week as a beggar, but it's not scalable. Mario will have no secret recipes, business skills, or a chain of restaurants to pass on to his children. It's also a loss for that passerby, who unwisely gave his dollar to the beggar. In two years, that passerby is going to live in an apartment with no good place to eat within walking distance. "Where are all the restaurateurs?" he wonders.

In a different future, the empanada business has done so well that a second branch opens up next to the apartment. Not only that, but one day our passerby is in that restaurant, enjoying the tasty food, when a woman walks in to eat. She sits across from him and they strike up a conversation. As they speak, a song plays over the radio. It will become 'their song.' Months later, the couple will be making love while this artist's album plays on the speaker. Our passerby recognizes another song… yes… He's certain he heard it once, long ago. Oh my god! It's that guitar player in the subway! There was a beggar on the stairs going down to catch the train, but he held on to his last loose bill. Then, he heard this guy play next to the tracks. Wow! The passerby felt compelled to support the artistry that was coming out of that guitar. Thankfully, enough other people made the same decision. That poor musician was able to afford a studio to cut his debut EP. One of the songs blew up, and he became a household name. How many joyful moments have since been had (at wedding parties, romantic vacations, and holiday gatherings) while dancing to the contagious rhythms of "Amor para todos"?

Once upon a time, I lived in Colombia, working as an English teacher. On the way to my school I passed plenty of panhandlers, but there were also some enterprising souls. I noticed the beggars' situations never changed over the course of the year. They mostly squatted in the same spots, wore the same clothes, and had not developed any direction or momentum from the money they accrued.

On the other hand, there was a young man who boarded my bus a few times a week. He gave a fantastic presentation about his wafers. There was always a special promotion. Typically, if you bought two packets of the chocolate flavor, you'd get one of the strawberry for free. I admired his pluck. Munching on the sweet wafers made the arduous journey, down Bogota's traffic-choked streets, a little more enjoyable. I would enthusiastically greet the kid, tell him how much I loved his product, and often buy extra for people in the office. Over the year, his business grew. He was eventually able to employ a sister. I'd like to think he invested some of that money in other ideas and lifted his family into a better spot. This is the energy I want to support directly.

BRAD PITT MOMENT

But, it's still tough when you walk by the beggar. It feels cold to look the other way, even if you know your money won't help. The good news is, there is something you can give freely. Something that will enhance their condition and yours as well. Perhaps, for just a moment. Perhaps, for much longer. One of the most influential people in my life was a guy I knew for less than 2 minutes. He gave me that thing.

I was working as a grocery bagger for Thompson's Food Basket in Peoria, IL. One day, a cashier called in sick and I was asked to work the register.

I was a super shy kid. My family had moved back to the United States after 7 years in Asia. I had trouble adjusting to the new social dynamics at school. I became the nerdy, introverted type who was often picked on by high status kids. I generally kept my gaze down, because to look up could invite trouble.

As customers came through the check-out line that day, I greeted them without eye contact. I'd scan their items with a minimum of conversation. Just the basics. I was hiding in plain sight. All day long people went along with this dynamic, treating me as a faceless service provider. Then, someone didn't.

"Hey, how's it going?" I said, not looking up as I reached for this man's items.

"I'm good, brother. How are you?" His voice came down from a head that only appeared in my peripheral vision.

"Good," I said rotely, not looking up, as I reached to scan a carton of eggs.

"No, man," he said in a firm but personable tone, "How's it going?"

Everything stopped. It was clear that this dude was going to stand there until I engaged. He was holding the space.

I lifted my gaze up, suddenly very aware and present. There was a man in the prime of his life. He looked like Brad Pitt in Fight Club: handsome, fit, and vibrant. He had all of his attention focused upon me. His eyes danced playfully, but unlike the school bullies, I wasn't being set up for something cruel. He was inviting me forward.

"Oh... I guess I'm good," I stammered.

"Right on," replied the guy with a warm smile, still looking at me.

We finished the transaction and he went his way. I never saw him again.

That's my story. This happened over 30 years ago. It still makes me misty. A super cool, alpha dude gave me all his attention for a moment. He acknowledged me: a shy, skinny, socially awkward 16-year-old, who still hadn't kissed a girl. For a moment, I wasn't just a bumbling kid that handled groceries for minimum wage. I was a fellow human being. I was a bro. Because of him, I try to take a small moment to acknowledge the people around me. I intend to look everyone in the eye and say (silently or out loud), "Hello." When I approach someone in a transactional environment (barista, server, receptionist at the hotel), the first beat is to greet them as a person. The second beat is about the thing I want.

Now, imagine if this dude in the grocery store had treated me as every other customer had, with nominal attention; but, on his way out, he handed me a 10$ tip. That would be a lot of money for a kid working minimum wage in the 80s. Would it have any impact on my life a month later? Probably not. Better if he gave that 10$ to the guitar player in the subway station or to a charity that buys malaria nets for children in Africa. He gave me the thing I really needed.

What this man did for me, you can do for everyone in the world, including the panhandlers. Have you ever observed a beggar from a distance? Notice how few people look at them. Folks, passing by, are afraid they will get locked in, or feel guilty, or invite trouble. Of those who hand over money, most don't turn towards the other. What if, instead of looking away, we made eye contact? What if we smiled and said, "Hello"? What if we took a beat to feel our shared humanity? This could be done in 2 seconds, without breaking stride. Or, you could stop for a while and listen to their story. Everyone wants to be heard and acknowledged. The guy on the street also has these needs.

HOLDING BOUNDARIES WITH SHIVA

Ah, but the fear! "If I look at them, they will pull me into their orbit. They are going to tell me a sad story and then ask for money. Then, I'm either going to have to give them cash, or feel like an asshole. It's just going to be awkward."

These concerns, which I know well, came to me often. Then, I worked through the priorities listed above. I am now certain, in almost all cases, there is a better place to put my money than into the hand of a random stranger. If I were to give money to a stranger, it would be my choice, not theirs. But let's say they press the issue, which is common. Now they are giving me an excellent opportunity to hold a boundary. This is a skill we all should master in life. All kinds of bad actors are coming for you if you can't hold a boundary. If you can't hold a "No" with a panhandler, the first con man (or selfish lover) you encounter is going to take advantage of you. This is your boundary holding dojo. Can you be friendly, engaged, and also set a limit to where the interaction will go?

A man came straight up to me in the Kali-ghat neighborhood of Kolkata. He wore an expression like he was an old friend who encountered me after a long absence. Did I know this guy?

"Today, I went to the temple," he said, "and Shiva told me I would meet you. He told me that you were the man who would help me."

"Why didn't Shiva give me some advanced notice about this?" I thought to myself, "This is an interesting angle. Either the man has a very unique schtick, or he is deranged."

My friend and I had just ordered an Uber, which was going to take five minutes to arrive. I had nothing pressing to do in that short span of time, so I decided to give this man my full attention, but not my money. Khali-ghat is a crowded place, full of beggars and touts. Many of them were watching this interaction unfold. If I pulled my wallet out, it was guaranteed that a mob of others would form, each explaining how their needs were more desperate. Between my friend and I, there would not be enough cash to satisfy the demand that would suddenly come our way. A mood of anger would be more likely than one of appeasement. It was imperative to hold my boundary on the money, which, of course, he probed a few times.

The man complained about society and the unfairness of it all. He scorned the "khaki men" who would not help him out financially. I listened. I looked him in the eyes. I sympathized with his frustrations. Life can give us some shitty hands of cards. He clearly had one. Also, banking on a savior was probably not a good strategy. My recommendation, delivered as gently as possible, was to stop expecting someone else to rescue him. The khaki men have their own worries to deal with. I asked how he could help himself. What changes could he make that might improve his situation?

What I hoped to give the man, before the Uber arrived, was a shift in perception. Although he undoubtedly had some difficult challenges to overcome, a victim's perspective was not serving him. It doesn't serve anyone. Did our conversation make a difference? Maybe. Not a rupee was given, yet we parted ways smiling and wishing each other well. He looked happy and energized from our interaction. I hope he went on to make some positive headway in his life.

Sometimes, in different environments, the spirit has moved me to more action. I've bought people meals, grabbed a blanket out of my apartment and laid it over a guy sleeping on the sidewalk, and offered plenty of hugs. There is a myriad of things one could do, but always remember: You have limited time, energy, and money. If you flood water into that particular canal, what things, downstream, are not going to get it? If you can't help out your best friend in a moment of need, because you gave your resources to some stranger on the street, you probably didn't think through your priorities enough.

THE DROWNING CHILD

There is a classic hypothetical of a man walking down the street in a new suit who notices a small boy drowning in a marsh to the side of the road. He is able to wade into the shallow water and pull the boy out, but his suit is ruined. Of course, we would expect this man to make the trade-off. If he allowed the boy to die in order to preserve his clothes, we'd call him a monster. I'm assuming you would not only sacrifice your suit to save the child, but you'd also feel very good about the whole interaction. It might be one of your proudest life moments.

The process of donating 100$ to provide malaria nets for small children is also an inconvenience (like wading into a swamp) and a cost (like ruining a new suit). We don't expect anyone to do it, and it would certainly not provide the same level of good feels as rescuing a drowning boy. However, that 100$ might save multiple kids.

There is something genetic at work here. Something that has carried over from our pre-agriculture days. Just as we have a habit of overeating at a buffet (a daydream fantasy for a forager), stew in murderous rage over someone who cut us off in traffic, and have a propensity to create out-groups (covered in Aha! 3), it makes total sense that a hunter/gatherer would not care at all for a human who lives on a different continent. They would never know of their existence, nor could they do anything helpful if they did.

Today, obviously, we do know about lives far away, we can affect those lives, and we are interconnected in a way that cannot be ignored. Most of humanity's great existential threats cannot be solved by a single friend group or even a single nation. When it comes to charity, it's wise to turn the volume down on feelings and turn it up on other metrics. Here is where something called Effective Altruism comes in. It's a relatively new movement, which encourages a focus on problems that are:

- Great in scale (it affects many lives, by a great amount)

- Highly neglected (few other people are working on addressing the problem)

- Highly solvable or tractable (additional resources will do a great deal to address it)

I would encourage you to look into this subject at effectivealtruism.org.

HORSES AND WATER

Broadly speaking, as you become a seasoned traveler, you will begin to see angles that the untraveled do not. You'll meet people who have never left their fishbowls, and therefore lack the multicultural perspective that you have gathered. You may come to care for some of these people and want to help them out. You will see ways they could immediately improve their situation.

Offering advice is a generous thing to do. It's kind-hearted to invest your time and energy into helping someone improve their life. If that person fails to take the baton and run with your advice, or take any action towards solving the issue, it's foolish to put any more of your effort into the cause.

Everyone needs to put in the work in life. There is no magic bullet. If you want a strong body, you've got to sweat through the exercise. If you want a calm mind, you've got to train it. If you want to change your relationships, you've got to change how you relate. Any transformation requires effort and sacrifice. Something new means something old must be released. If you want six pack abs, the tubs of ice cream must go. If you want a creative project to come to life, the video game addiction must be laid on the altar. Nobody can do this for you.

Some folks don't see the problem clearly, but when it's pointed out, they are ready to do that work. Some folks don't want to do the work. Some folks want someone to do it for them. Some want to cling to a victim status. Some need to see the bottom of the barrel before they are ready to head up. You'll meet all these characters in your travels. Have empathy for everyone. Help only the ones who are ready to do the work.

The truth is, we know this intimately, because we've been on the other side of this glass. I've received a lot of good advice in my life that I didn't take. I just wasn't ready for it. I was lost in a story that wouldn't accommodate that advice, or I didn't want to let go of something that was hindering me. I had to live out my karma, just as others must live theirs out.

This brings up some interesting questions. If you put this shoe on the other foot, how are you resisting good advice?

Ponder this:

❯ Have you tried to "save" people in the past who were not willing to be saved? What did you learn from that experience?

❯ Have you received advice recently that you haven't acted on? Why? Was it unwise, or does it require work and sacrifice that you are reluctant to do?

❯ Do you take a moment to warmly acknowledge people in casual encounters? How does it feel? Can you hold a boundary if someone tries to push the interaction farther than your level of comfort?

❯ Have you considered Lynne Twist's questions?

   ▸ Which artists would you like to support because their creations hold intrinsic, critical value?

   ▸ What are your passions and how can you financially support them?

   ▸ Where could you alleviate the most amount of suffering in the world, in the most effective manner?

You, the rational traveler, have come to the sad but true realization that you cannot save everyone. Handing out cash indiscriminately is generally a bad idea. Placing kind attention on others is a wonderful thing to do. By allocating resources wisely, you can cause the most effective and positive change in the world.

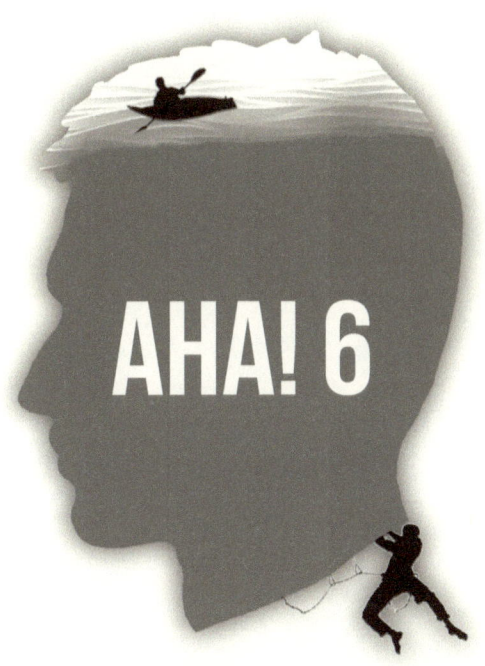

YOU ARE GOING TO DIE.

....

We live in a culture where it has been rubbed into us in every conceivable way that to die is a terrible thing. And that is a tremendous disease from which our culture in particular suffers.

~ Alan Watts

The irony of man's condition is that the deepest need is to be free of the anxiety of death and annihilation; but it is life itself which awakens it, and so we must shrink from being fully alive.

~ Ernest Becker

*W*e stood in a semicircle and stared at each other. Who would attempt to drive the heavy vehicle down this massive dune? If it got stuck again, we would all die.

The whole situation was absurd. Idiotic. We'd just filmed for several days in California's remote Mojave Desert. All precautions were taken. There was a backup SUV, in case the on-camera vehicle got stuck. There were tow straps. Both vehicles were stuffed with gallons of water and emergency survival gear. Yet here we were, ten days later, on top of this lonely dune, 50 miles to the nearest road with half a can of Diet Coke in the cupholder. Our phones had no signal. It was pitch dark. Our robust FJ Cruiser sat like a beached whale, buried to the chassis.

Rush. Of course, it was a mindless rush to get something done. An opportunity to speed up the schedule appeared, and, eager to finish our episode, we seized it. The final location for this day was a legal brothel. The ladies gave us a small tour of the facility, explained how prostitution was regulated in Nevada, and helped us film a funny little sequence for the show.

After saying our goodbyes I stepped outside and noticed the setting sun, still hovering a couple of hands above the horizon. The official plan was to return to Las Vegas, a few hours away, and then come back north in the morning to get our final desert scene. But we were close to that location now, and if we moved real fast, we could get there with a few rays of sunshine to spare.

I sped down a lonely two-lane road and then turned onto a dirt track. The way became progressively more and more primitive as we approached a series of giant sand dunes. Soon, I left the dirt road entirely and cut across the open desert towards the location. It would be there, I had determined, that an old wagon full of whiskey had disappeared 150 years ago. It was a true missing treasure. There was no reasonable hope of finding it, but I believed it could be somewhere underneath the biggest dune. Getting the final shot in front of that dune, in the golden light of the setting sun, would be a perfect ending to our Nevada episode.

We rolled up as the sun began kissing the horizon. I jumped out of the driver's seat, already wearing a mic. The crew hopped out with cameras rolling. We got it! Episode done! In a state of high elation, I kicked off my cowboy boots and ran up the dune.

"Meet me up there!" I hollered back.

The crew decided to give our production car a real test. Why not? It had to be returned soon. We had still not ridden it to the limit. They plowed up the sand at a ridiculously steep angle. The SUV reached a little plateau atop the dune and then the tires started spinning.

"Stop!" I yelled, watching the car dig itself in.

It was too late. By the time the cameraman took his foot off the gas, the vehicle had sunk into a gritty grave. Within minutes it was a pitch dark night. The Milky Way glittered crystal clear above. A few meters to the side, nothing was visible. We all turned on our cell phone flashlights and *assessed the situation. The walk was too far without fluids. We had to get that car out.*

Everyone got on their bellies and began digging. For hours we scooped the bottom of the SUV clear. I walked the perimeter and found some tumbleweed to stuff under the tires for better grip. Then, we debated on who would attempt to drive the car out. Any mistake could doom the crew.

"I'll do it," I said, and took the keys.

Putting the car in reverse I eased on the accelerator, feeling carefully for any loss of traction in the tires. The rubber held. The formidable SUV tilted off the plateau and made it onto the downward slope. After a few more tricky maneuvers on the descent we hit the harder packed sand below. We were free, yet the possibility of our demise in that desert, due to a stupid oversight, sticks with me.

This close call wasn't my only brush with death in life. I've almost been smashed by two separate buses in the Philippines, nearly avoided a handful of motorcycle accidents, been sucked into a Brazilian cumulus nimbus on a paraglider, had a house-sized boulder roll right in front of my van in Nepal, and damn near drowned in a couple of riptides. Moreover, I've seen death around me all over the world, including burning corpses on the banks of the Ganges.

The conscious traveler has also seen the Grim Reaper at work. They have observed how people around the world deal with the demise of life, from grief to celebration. What the traveler witnesses the most, however, is denial. We mindlessly move through the motions of our lives without paying full attention, assuming there will always be a new moment in front of us. It's an illusion, but I fall into it all the time. I'm often not fully committed to the thing that's happening now (the company of a friend, the taste of the food I'm eating, the sensations in my body as I jog). My mind is lost in thought. Inherent in this process is an underappreciation of the present. The good news is that there is a way to push back.

THE GRIM ELEPHANT IN THE ROOM

In the late 1960s, the first written warnings appeared on cigarette packs. By the early 2000s, graphic images went global. You've probably seen those gnarly pictures. Who would want to risk that? It turns out, almost everyone. According to a 2021 study[9], this entire effort, "did not affect either cigarette cessation or consumption levels." How does this make sense?

Earnest Becker, in his Pulitzer Prize winning book *The Denial of Death*, posits that all of society is constructed on a refusal to accept our finitude. On a personal level, immortality projects, hedonism, busyness, and entertainment all serve to push death away. It's that pushing that makes sense of the ineffective cigarette warnings. If the smoker were to actually acknowledge the warning, they would have to acknowledge their own mortality. We are just not interested in this consideration.

The habit of death denial is especially salient in modern consumer culture. The promise of immortality is big business. The beauty

---

[9] a b c Effect of Graphic Warning Labels on Cigarette Packs on US Smokers' Cognitions and Smoking Behavior After 3 Months. A Randomized Clinical Trial. David R. Strong, PhD1,2; John P. Pierce, PhD1,2; Kim Pulvers, PhD3; et al

product industry pulled in nearly 500 billion dollars in 2020. A good portion of this money was spent to fight off the aging process, or, more specifically, the perception that we are aging. Growing old, in consumer culture, is shameful. Signs of autumn are an unacceptable reminder that winter is coming for us all. Perhaps this is why we hide our elderly away in the United States.

In his book *Four Thousand Weeks*, Oliver Burkeman suggests that the appeal of social networks, which commodify our attention, is strangely related to death. Why is it so easy to doomscroll Instagram or Tik Tok; but it's so hard to put time into the projects we most care about? Perhaps you've long wanted to write a book, learn Portuguese, or start a small business. You know in your soul this project deserves top priority. So, why is the news/entertainment feed capturing so much of your time?

According to Burkeman, the big projects bring us into contact with our finitude and limitations. We might struggle, fail, or die before achieving the grand results we imagined. Nothing of value is guaranteed. This is scary. On the other hand, social feeds (and 24/7 news cycles) offer a limitless landscape. This is appealing.

The traveler has noticed that humanity wasn't always so estranged from their mortality. They have seen Day of the Dead celebrations in Mexico, watched the Koreans washing their ancestors' tombstones, and noticed Osiris in Egyptian reliefs. They've also walked through the Killing Fields of Cambodia, the cemetery of Verdun, and the ghats of Varanasi. They have understood that the blooming cherry blossoms in Japan are so celebrated because their beauty is temporary, like life itself. With all this information, the conscious traveler has come to accept their mortality and savor their life all the more.

LOOK ON MY WORKS AND DESPAIR!

In contemporary culture, it's the living who are celebrated. Did you hear about the mega-yacht that the tech CEO just bought? Did you see the dress that the reality star wore to the awards show? Did you read about the affair the top athlete is having with the model? The gossip, celebrity, and news cycles are consumed with what's fresh. Most of humanity's great lessons, however, must be seen at a distance.

Travelers are typically less invested in the modern cultural icons of a foreign land and more interested in its historical ones. Very few people travel to Egypt to learn about their Kardashians, but they would like to know about the Pharaohs. Only a handful of people come to Peru to learn about their boy bands, but many are curious about the Incas. Once you step away from your home, you quickly become aware of how unimportant pop culture becomes when it's not your culture.

Distance presents the conscious traveler with a unique question, "When the sands of time have worn off the hype, the power, and the mystique; what is left?" There is evidence that early forms of football (soccer) were played more than 2,000 years ago in China, Greece, Rome, and parts of Central America. Could you name the Cristiano Ronaldo from that era? Does anyone care? How many Aztec and Sumerian leaders could be recalled by the average Joe or Jane? The poem *Ozymandias* by Shelley captures the spirit of this point:

I met a traveller from an antique land
Who said: "Two vast and trunkless legs of stone
Stand in the desert . . . Near them, on the sand,
Half sunk, a shattered visage lies, whose frown,
And wrinkled lip, and sneer of cold command,
Tell that its sculptor well those passions read
Which yet survive, stamped on these lifeless things,
The hand that mocked them, and the heart that fed:
And on the pedestal these words appear:
'My name is Ozymandias, king of kings:
Look on my works, ye Mighty, and despair!'
Nothing beside remains. Round the decay
Of that colossal wreck, boundless and bare
The lone and level sands stretch far away.

Once upon a time, in this fictional world, people obviously shivered at the mention of the name "Ozymandias." In real history, there have been countless warlords, generals, and kings who held a similar notoriety. Nobody cares enough to remember them now, because terror-inducing power loses its value through the gauntlet of time. Who was the richest citizen at the height of the Roman Empire? Who was the most beautiful woman in the Han Dynasty? Which singer, during the reign of the Mughals, had the most captivating voice? Nobody knows. Nobody cares. These contemporary measures of value lose their currency within a few centuries.

What seems to endure longest through the tunnel of time? Consider Shelly's poem, the tragedies of Shakespeare, the Pyramids of Giza, Michelangelo's David, Plato's Republic, the Bhagavad Gita, the Torah, On the Origin of Species, and Venus of Willendorf.

Insightful and inspirational art are mediums that capture the nature of the human condition. Philosophy and science help us understand our place in the universe. These things continue to be appreciated because they continue to offer society something useful. With this in mind even the most resolute narcissist, if thinking rationally, would be wise to put some effort into creating a work that transcends his ego. Humanity keeps these kinds of treasures in its chest, while every other endeavor will eventually be forgotten.

BAD MAN INCINERATION

Regardless of creating a monumental work of science, philosophy, or art; the life of a person will continue, namelessly, through future generations long after their demise. In my travels, I have seen how the deaths of bad people and good people have scattered different waves of energy in their wake. The former group often leaves families and communities with unresolved trauma. There is a wound in the place of the apology, the embrace, or the "I love you" that never came, and never will. Good people are grieved with a different strain of tears, testimonies of gratitude, and hearts full of appreciation. The good person built community in their life. In their death, that community comes together to reaffirm the values and the virtues which attracted them to this person.

In Bali, I witnessed hundreds of villagers coming together in a celebration of life, over the death of one good man. It was the most wonderful funeral I've ever seen. I met several lovely people during the long ceremony, which ended in the man's public cremation. One of those people was a young father who brought his daughter to the event. He wanted her to understand that this was an inescapable aspect of life, and to develop a healthy relationship with the idea of death. He also told me that not every funeral on the island was like this one. "If a man leads a selfish life and doesn't treat others with respect and kindness, he will be lucky if his wife and children show up at the mortuary to witness his incineration," he told me with a solemn look.

I feel some sympathy for the souls who got the lonely funeral. Many of them surely had the ambition to one day right the wrongs. They were planning to do all those things that their heart told them they should. They just thought they had more time. They didn't know that morning, at breakfast, would be the last chance to say something to their wife and daughter. They didn't know that the changes they wanted to make could not wait for one more day.

TOOLS TO SEE THE REAPER

So how do we regain a visceral relationship to our finitude? How can we fully savor this short life and remain fully awake and attentive to the small moments? How can we prepare ourselves to leave smiling when the ride is over? The conscious traveler has, perhaps, already seen the jigsaw pieces scattered across the landscape.

- **History as a reminder** - When I stand in the ruins of an old structure, I consider how many people have come before me: The laborers who built it, the original occupants, the first archeologists to discover it, the first tourists to visit. I imagine what their experience must have been. Then, I recall that they are all dead. I will soon join their company. One more person in that old castle, fortress, or temple who will be forgotten. One day, no one on the planet will remember my sense of humor, how I drank my coffee, or the sound of my voice.

This is an easy exercise to employ when you are staring at old photographs or portrait paintings in museums. These people held similar concerns as you and I do. Generally speaking, they hoped for the same things. They had loves, rivalries, grievances, self-doubt, hope for the future, erotic thoughts, sadness, and moments of great joy. Where is any of that now? Specifically, I like to think of all the worries they carried, perhaps unnecessarily. It was such a brief moment in time they had to savor. If I could send a message back, I'd say, "Enjoy it. Try things. Be brave. Love fearlessly." What message would you send back?

● **Collective wisdom** - We are soaking in the zeitgeist, the spirit of our time. It's the attitudes, beliefs, and assumptions of our era, which hold us inside a certain bubble. The thing is, most people aren't consciously aware of this fish tank because they have never left it. The conscious traveler, however, has peered into other containers, from other places and eras. While the present zeitgeist here in the United States, where I currently sit, gives scant thought to mortality, this is not true of other locations and eras.

  ▶ **The last time** - Once more, let's dip into stoic wisdom. The old Greeks and Romans understood their finitude very well. An exercise encouraged by these philosophers is loosely called the "Last Time Meditation."

This past fall, I was hiking down a leisurely trail in central Serbia. A thought percolated up, "Wow… you've hiked so many trails in your life. This is pretty easy for you." To be honest, it was a judgment of the trail. I had traveled a couple of hours to get there, only to feel underwhelmed by the difficulty. It wasn't challenging enough. Then, suddenly, my perspective shifted.

I remembered this stoic technique. I considered that tomorrow I could suffer a terrible accident and lose my ability to walk. It happens to people every day. What if this was the last time I would amble freely through a forest? With this new perspective, the whole hike changed. I relished in my body's ability to move over the terrain. I felt awe at the sight of the natural beauty as my able legs glided through the lush foliage.

There will indeed be a last time I eat pumpkin pie, say goodbye to a friend, drive the I-405, hear a Michael Franti song, sleep in a tent, and watch a sunrise. Most likely, I will have no clue when this last time is happening. I will be playing tennis under the assumption that I will play tennis again one day. But I won't. It will be the last time. If I realized that, I would probably soak it up a little more. Maybe I'm playing tennis with my friend Mark. I'm going to assume I'll see him again. But I won't. It will be the last time. If I realized that, I'd probably be a little nicer and more attentive to him. How to solve this conundrum? Treat every one of these moments as if it were the last time.

For the traveler, this is an easy exercise to do as you leave home for your next journey. You hope to be back. But you might not be. You hope everyone will be there when you are back. But they might not be. Think about that when you say your goodbyes. Give those moments a little more attention. They could be the last time.

▶ **Eastern philosophy** - It was in Japan that I was first exposed to the ideas of Zen Buddhism. It felt like a portal to another universe had opened up. Now, I start each day with a vipassana, non-dualistic, meditation. At its core, it teaches me that everything is transitory and in process, including Jonathan Legg. With time, one gradually develops an ability to drop back and observe the flow of thoughts, feelings, and sensations without reaction. The more free I become from the drama playing in my head, the more I'm able to be present for the life in front of me and the people I love.

Here is one particular meditation technique I find beneficial from Jon Kabat-Zinn's *Wherever You Go, There You Are*: Sitting in a place where you are anonymous and surrounded by others (like a park bench), imagine that you are dead. Jon writes, "If you did die, all your responsibilities and obligations would immediately evaporate. Their residue would somehow get worked out without you. No one else can take over your unique agenda. It would die or peter out with you just as it has for everyone else who has ever died. So you don't need to worry about it in any absolute way. If this is true, maybe you don't need to make one more phone call right now, even if you think you do. Maybe you don't need to read something just now, or run one more errand. By taking a few moments to "die on purpose" to the rush of time while you are still living, you free yourself to have time for the present. By "dying" now, in this way, you actually become more alive now."

▸ **Momento mori** - The conscious traveler has noticed a theme that's predominant in medieval European architecture and art. The memento mori (reminder of death) is most commonly expressed as a skull. Other motifs include coffins, hourglasses, bones, and wilting flowers. The idea, again, is impermanence. Time is sacred. Don't waste it on pettiness. Do the most important thing now. Say the words now.

⟩ **Connecting to the tree** - We are so far out on our branch now. So far, we don't really notice it anymore. The traveler will, at one point, glimpse the leaves shimmering far away and make the realization: They are connected to the Tree of Life. In the behavior of the chimpanzees in Tanzania or in the expressions of the bonobos south of the Congo River, it's easy to tell. These creatures are not so dissimilar. But, in the plants and fungus, it is harder to feel our distant relationship… until you consume them.

The Mazatec people of Oaxaca did an amazing thing. They preserved the knowledge of psilocybe cubensis in the Americas, when the West had all but forgotten about them. How could we forget? Our earliest ancestors painted them on the cave walls as a reminder. But we forgot, nonetheless. Then, in the mid 50s an American banker, Gordon Wasson, traveled to this region of Mexico to participate in a ritual. When he returned, he published an account of his experience. The groundbreaking photo essay in *Life* magazine brought the lost awareness back. It was titled "Seeking the Magic Mushroom."

In the article, Gordon recounts his experience after consuming the sacrament: "The visions were not blurred or uncertain. They were sharply focused, the lines and colors being so sharp that they seemed more real to me than anything I had ever seen with my own eyes. I felt that I was now seeing plain, whereas ordinary vision gives us an imperfect view; I was seeing the archetypes, the Platonic ideas, that underlie the imperfect images of everyday life. The thought crossed my mind: could the divine mushrooms be the secret that lay behind the ancient mysteries?"

Sixty years later, I followed in Gordon's footsteps, participating in a similar ritual in a rural village above Huautla de Jimenez. I can verify that his account rings true to my experience. Let me add something. Gordon took the mushrooms in a hut. Had the American banker taken these mushrooms in the wilderness, by the light of day, he would have had additional perspectives. He would have seen the artificial boundary between "I" and "not I" begin to dissolve. The feeling of being a lonely capsule of flesh, trudging through a hostile world, may have lifted like a fog.

CAVE ART SHOWING A BEE-FACED SHAMAN HOLDING MUSHROOMS 4,000 - 9,000 BC
IMAGE FROM TERENCE MCKENNA'S **FOOD OF THE GODS**

The town of Eleusis, just 30 kilometers from Athens, was the site of the ancient world's most enduring and powerful ritual. The so-called "Eleusinian Mysteries" lasted almost 2000 years. Every Greek participated in this ceremony once in their lives. Although the details were kept relatively secret over the eons, research revealed in Brian Muraresku's *The Immortality Key* offers some fascinating revelations. Tripping on the fungi ergot (from which LSD was later synthesized), the ancient Greeks experienced Persephone's descent and reemergence from the underworld. The most important and enduring ritual in the ancient world revolved around a psychedelic experience of death and rebirth.

In the rainforests of Peru, the Shipibo-Conibo carry a similar tradition. The plant that connects them to the tree of life, death, and rebirth, is called ayahuasca. Consuming a small cup of this plant's juice gave me the most profound night of my adulthood. It was as if a grandmotherly spirit pushed open all the chambers of my life so we could examine them together from a gentle, kind, and truthful perspective. It wouldn't be a stretch to say that one Jonathan Legg went into that ceremony and a different Jonathan left.

THE DEATH OF BORACAY

When you think about it, change is essentially the death of one thing that gets replaced by another. It's constantly in process with us and the world we inhabit. What happened to Jonathan Legg, the child, who could play with his Masters of the Universe figures for hours? That kid essentially left this world when the teenage Jonathan Legg was born. In this manner, you are dying and being reborn all the time.

Have you ever returned to a special spot many years later? Perhaps it was a remote beach hamlet on a Thai island with a virgin strip of sand. There was only one place to stay: a rustic set of bungalows that blended into the forest surrounding a picturesque cove. You spent a romantic week there with a lover, skinny-dipping in the sea at night with the stars above. You pulled coconuts off the trees and hiked to a distant waterfall that was so remote you felt like the first person to discover it. The thing to remember, as you savor this spot, is that it is ephemeral. Like the Japanese cherry blossom, it will not last forever.

A decade later, you decide to return, hoping to recapture some of that old magic. On arrival, to your chagrin, the beach is full of sunbathers and all their accouterments: beach blankets, coolers, and floaties for the children. They sit on recliners under the shade of umbrellas. Both are provided by the adjacent row of hotels which stand where native trees once grew. The hotels share space with convenient stores, restaurants, and bars blasting the latest pop music from their open doors. Everyone there seems to be having a great time, except for you. Why is that? They came for the beach that is alive. You came for the one that is dead.

The happy people, in this overdeveloped town, either never knew the pristine, non-touristy beach from a decade earlier, or they let it go. Trying to capture the same magic twice, in the same place, is a difficult feat. It often ends in disappointment. Everything is changing. Only the memory can stay the same. I had to learn this lesson many times before I came up with a few rules for myself.

- If I make a wonderful memory in a special place, especially a location that is prone to change completely, I often never return there. The moment and the location are married in my mind. I want to leave that memory just as it is. There are plenty of other destinations in which to have new adventures.

- When planning to travel to a new destination, contrary to most advice, do *the least* amount of research possible. In the days before Instagram, I would read the flowery descriptions written in guidebooks and begin to form a mental picture of a location. All too often, the destination would not pair with the construct I had in my mind and I'd find myself disappointed.

  Now, with pictures and videos on the socials, the letdowns can be more severe. This media is edited to look as spectacular as possible. Influencers wake up at 5 a.m. to get shots without the crowds. This content sets the bar high. Keep it low by doing the bare minimum of preparation for your trip. This is similar to my movie trailer policy. Once you've decided you're going to see a movie, it's best to stop watching the preview. Any additional viewing just takes away an element of surprise. Better to come into the film with no idea of where it's going.

- I generally choose places that are not overly lauded as "must sees" or five-star sites. A better time has consistently been had on the fringes and in three-star locations.

JAPANESE RICE

When I lived in Japan, the route from home to the train station passed by fields of rice. In winter they were barren, and in early spring the ground was tilled and straw was mixed into the soil. A while later, the fields would be full of water. Then, one day, tiny seedlings would be planted. These seedlings grew full and lush throughout the summer until the time of the harvest.

The morning commuters from my neighborhood observed this whole process unfold. A process that denoted the changing of seasons. They also participated in these shifts. There are annual festivals and events, closely linked to the time of year, which all citizens know. During one magic weekend in the spring, everybody posts up in a park under the cherry blossom trees to savor the flowering of new life. In the summer there will be hanabi (fireworks) that celebrate the flourishing of life. These traditions root the people to everything that is happening around them in nature. They are constantly reminded of the changing, yet circular, quality of existence. Every time one thing ends, another begins.

Japan has an old culture that has been historically insular. This secluded island-nation has marinated its citizens in the slow cooking, closed-pot, stew of its culture. The traditions, therefore, permeate into the bones of the people. By contrast, the United States is a bit like a few minutes in the microwave. To use a better metaphor, if America were a boat, its keel would not penetrate very deep into the water. It's not seriously committed to a certain direction (other than, perhaps, rugged individualism and self-enrichment). It can be shifted around more easily. There is much less crossover with the activities of the past and those of the present. Young Americans participate in few of the things their parents did at that age.

Both countries, and indeed the entire world, have now entered into a unique era of rapid change. Technology, which has grown to dominate our day to day, has an evergreen, endless quality. Unlike the familiar and well-worn traditions of the past, often linked to the seasons, media is always new and fresh. This cornucopia of novel content makes the old ways feel outdated. Many folks, especially living in urban environments, have disconnected from the rituals their ancestors practiced for millennia.

Not everyone on the globe has entered this new era from the same starting point. A young girl from Kyusu, or boy from a Basque village, has been handed a ship with a deep keel. They have a backbone of traditions to lean on. They have something stable and enduring in a generation of instability and change. A kid from Toronto, raised without many traditions, is navigating into the choppy waters of this exciting yet discombobulating time on a shifty vessel.

How rooted and stable do you feel right now? How much anxiety are you carrying that might have a connection to the uncertainty of the future? I've lived a life about as free as a man can, but now am questioning the virtue of having no anchors or constraints. Total freedom is inherently a chaotic environment. Perhaps, committing to certain rituals and traditions, linked to the passage of time, places us in a rhythm with the spinning planet, the swirling cosmos, and the company of our long line of ancestors. As good as it feels to be free, it might feel even better to be aligned.

LUNA MADRE

A seasoned traveler has witnessed a vast array of traditions that they could choose to honor, if they wished. However, perhaps none as powerful as the ones from their own past. Whatever your great grandparents celebrated and honored might be worth a second look. The mythology surrounding these traditions could be harder for us to swallow in any literal sense, but does it matter?

There are universals which have been recognized since the dawn of *Homo sapien*. The cycle of the moon is probably the oldest of these. Long before our species spread out from the motherland of Africa and into the latitudes of four seasons, the changing moonlight went hand in hand with activities and traditions. It is the original marker of time. Why not harness this celestial clock to bookmark and reflect upon your life?

What if, on every full moon, you dedicated just 30 minutes thinking about your situation and to write something in a journal? Note what kind of progress you've made on the things you'd like to achieve. Write down the high moments from the previous cycle in order to cultivate gratitude, and the low points in order to find the lessons. Reaffirm the story of who you are, what you stand for, and where you intend to go.

Beyond the moon, the seasons must be the next in line of seniority. Many religious holidays have been pasted on top of the solstices and equinoxes, which have existed long before anyone put a name to God. The balance of southern and northern hemispheres, as witnessed on the first day of spring, has been recognized long before anyone uttered the word "Easter." The solstices and equinoxes divide the year into quarters and signal a shift in energy. For tens of thousands of years, communities would completely adjust their daily activities in line with these shifts. Maybe it's worth recognizing these days in some way that is meaningful to you.

On a much smaller scale, the day itself has a cycle. If you hike up into the mountains with camping gear and spend a few nights in the wild, you will quickly sync up to nature's rhythm. Putting away the electronics, you will wake up with the sun, be drawn into activity during the day (with all the other diurnal animals), realize when it's time to seek shelter and make camp, and fall asleep as the cold of night descends.

Recently, I climbed to a peak in the Sierra mountains of central California. During the ascent, a warm breeze from the valley below blew up the trail. On top, I sat for a long moment, eating snacks and reflecting on life. Then, I noticed a subtle shift in the air. My shadow had grown long. It was time to descend. When I got back to the tent, a brisk wind was howling down the mountain. The day had its inhale and exhale. There was a time for me to go up and get something (the experience and the perspective) and a time to go down to reflect on the experience, integrate it, and share any new wisdom (as I'm doing right now in this paragraph).

Although most of my days are spent in urban environments, I'm trying to carry a bit of this natural cycle with me. There is a time to wake up and get natural light into my eyes, which signals the nervous system to begin daytime processes[10]. There is a time to exercise my body, to open up the emails and social feeds, and to drop into undistracted work. As the sun begins to set, screens get turned off and lights get dimmed. Again, it's the time to reflect, integrate, and share with your family and friends.

THE GIRL FROM AUSTRALIA

Travel has a unique way of shrinking time into bite size chunks. A person who never leaves their home town can easily fall into the illusion that they will live forever. When you've only got two weeks in Armenia, your Armenian life is clearly on the ticker. Unless you have family there, you'll probably never come back. Every changing destination puts the finitude of your time in better focus.

It's a similar case with travel romance. I once met a cool girl in the lobby of my hotel in Istanbul. After a small chat, three things were clear: There was electricity between us, she had a very similar route planned through Turkey, and she was returning to Australia in ten days. At home, two lovers might play cat and mouse for months. You don't want to appear too eager or needy. On the road, there is no time to waste. If it's on, it's on. She and I became like boyfriend and girlfriend for the following week. We opened up to each other. After she returned to Australia, we never spoke again; but, this soul-warming feeling, of being seen and appreciated, stuck with me (and I hope with her too). That was the good stuff.

---

[10] Andrew Huberman, a Neurobiologist at Stanford University, considers this the most important thing you can do in a day.

The lesson is, of course, that all of life could be lived this way, with a courageous openness to go deep when the signals feel right. There is no time to waste, ever. There is no guarantee that you don't have, right now, two weeks left wherever you are. Time is sacred. Act Accordingly.

Ponder this:

⊙ If you were to die today, how would you be remembered? What would the community say about you after you're gone? What have you left them that might carry on?

⊙ Do you have any practices that remind you of the finitude of time? Do you treat your time as sacred? If you did, what activities would you diminish and which ones would you amplify?

⊙ What rituals or traditions did your immediate ancestors honor? What purpose did they serve beyond any supernatural beliefs?

You, the attentive traveler, realize that everything is in a state of flow and change. This realization has now turned inward to the understanding and acceptance of your own mortality. This relationship with death augments your connection to life. You consider time sacred. Gazing at the ruins of past cultures becomes a reminder that most selfish endeavors are quickly forgotten, yet creative gifts to humanity transcend eras. You, the wise traveler, have incorporated traditions into your life that root and align it more closely to the flow of existence.

THE BEST LIVES ARE BUILT ON SERVICE, COMMUNITY, MEANINGFUL CHOICES, AND A LOT OF MESS

....

What should young people do with their lives today? Many things, obviously. But, the most daring thing is to create stable communities in which the terrible disease of loneliness can be cured.

~ Kurt Vonnegut

What does it profit a man to gain the whole world, yet forfeit his soul?

~ Mark 8:36

I had slipped into the Vinh Moc tunnels, near the central coast of Vietnam, and began sneaking around the huge labyrinth. Every now and then I passed a portal to the surface, where a cone of warm sunshine blazed down into the darkness. Occasionally, I'd hear voices up there and motion the small camera crew for silence. We had slipped in without notifying anyone, fearing that the complex might be officially closed or that we could be denied permission to film. Although I understand some criticisms of this guerilla filming practice, I've generally found that when shooting something raw, it's better to ask for forgiveness than permission. If a request enters the maze of bureaucratic authorization, things grind to a snail's pace (and entail the laborious submission of photocopies, official stamps, and completed forms). For a show based on spontaneous adventure, that basically equates to losing the opportunity entirely.

As I sneaked around the tunnels, I thought of the community who once lived down here. When American B-52s bombed this town relentlessly, the whole population moved underground. Despite not having a single engineer among them, they managed to survive for more than a year in this subterranean world, without losing a single life.

There is something even more remarkable. The most surprising detail was spoken to me by a young guide to the complex I encountered back on top. Her grandfather had endured that long bombardment in those dark tunnels below our feet.

"Could I meet him?" I inquired. "Would he be OK with an American?"

My father, while not directly involved in combat operations, was in Vietnam clearing roads for the army.

"Yes, no problem," she said, and went on to explain that her grandfather's philosophy was that there is no virtue to holding onto bitterness, but there was wisdom in remembering the lessons. In other words, forgive, but don't forget.

That her grandfather, and his compatriots, were able to forgive such a horrendous act of aggression is one the most remarkable feats of the heart I've ever heard.

Can you imagine a foreign military leveling your town? Your home, your community, everything you love and cherish turned into smoldering rubble. You and your family would live in mud tunnels for a year as explosions shook the earth around you. After that was over, how long would it take you to welcome citizens from that invading country back into your town as tourists and greet them with a smile?

I think there is a secret to the Vietnamese ability to pivot from grief, to hate, to forgiveness, and all the way to kindness. The secret is community. This realization came to me while I was speaking to a friend on his balcony high above Belgrade. As we gazed over the cityscape, he said that, as a kid, he stood on that same balcony and watched NATO bombs drop on his city. Then he turned to me with a wry smile and said, "You know, strangely, it was the best moment of my life." How could that be?

He went on to explain how the aggression brought the people together in a way that had never happened before or since. Suddenly, all the little gripes fell to the wayside. Your dog shit on my lawn, you occasionally walk with high heels on the floor above me, you didn't wave back to me that one time I waved to you... these petty concerns quickly evaporated when the bombs started to drop. There were much bigger fish to fry, and all hands were needed on that skillet. People gathered in plazas, hugging each other, encouraging each other, shouting affirmations of identity in unison, and singing songs of patriotism. Community is what gets you through the most challenging moments life can throw at you. Community can even make those moments pleasant in a best of times/ worst of times sort of way.

A LONELY CAVEMAN IS A DEAD CAVEMAN

The most grim and socially awkward people I've met in my travels have been, in some way, isolated. Some reasons for this condition are a lack of social skills, geographical separation, or a gross disparity of wealth. On the other hand, people in a community tend to smile more, open up to strangers faster, have more trust, hold less fear, sing more frequently, dance more often, and be more prone to laughter. A conscious traveler has noticed this pattern. They have determined that they too would be wise to invest in the endeavor of creating community and maintaining friendships.

Of course, from an evolutionary standpoint, this all makes good sense. For millions of years we woke up, hunted, gathered, ate, screwed, played, and fell back asleep next to 50 to 100 other humans. They were our family, best friends, and lovers. To be socially isolated meant you were shortly going to die. The plentiful array of predators, which prowled and slithered across the savanna, did not want to mess with a tribe of humans gathered around a fire with spears at the ready. But, they'd be more than happy to stalk a lone human with no backup.

This reality is baked into our genetic behavior to this day. Humans suffering from severe loneliness experience a series of micro-awakenings at night, because, when you are alone in the jungle, you must frequently survey your surroundings to check for impending danger. This is why loneliness has been associated with increased blood pressure, heart disease, depression, cognitive decline, and mortality.

When agriculture came on the scene, just 12,000 years ago, things began to quickly change for our species. Our perception of nature rapidly flipped. It was once a place of bounty. There was always fruit, nuts, and edible plants to gather; and often prey to hunt. Humans roamed through this terrain freely. Then suddenly, they stopped moving. There was one fixed field of wheat that they had to defend tooth and nail. Nature became a threatening force that had to be constantly beaten back. The rabbits and deer, which once were the hunter's prey, became the farmer's antagonists. If they got to your crop, you and your family might starve.

We began storing food, as it had to last until the next harvest. This stash had to be defended. Now fortifications and a soldier class emerged. This was essentially the beginning of the classic phrase,

"Get off my property." Weather had to cooperate exactly as planned, or, again, you and your family might starve. This might have constituted a shift in beliefs and the beginning of religious sacrifice. You'd do anything for that rain to come or for that frost to melt.

Unless you are waking up in Tanzania with your Hadza family, or reading this on Sentinel Island, you are a descendent of these farmers. This is why we carry elevated fears of the natural world. Consider that a film about a group of people in the wilderness is usually a thriller or a horror. This is a perspective born of agriculturists.

Then, the industrial revolution, less than 300 years ago, sped up the division between us, our communities, and the natural world. We traveled to cities seeking work and opportunity, leaving family and old friends behind. Now, here we are in the digital revolution, where life can essentially be conducted from behind a screen.

The rub is this: Our hardware has not kept pace. The last update to our physical brains has been at least 40,000 years ago, way before the agricultural revolution. Our melons are optimized for a hunter/gatherer tribal lifestyle, not our current circumstances. So, the anxiety you might feel in this modern world is quite understandable. When I witness a lost soul wandering down an alley, ranting at the air, I often think, "Of course." That's a natural reaction to very unnatural circumstances. How most of us hold it together is quite a feat.

Author Christopher Ryan, in *Civilized to Death*, makes the case that we are no longer living in our natural environment, but rather a kind of zoo that society has constructed around us. The big question, he poses to the reader, is: Do you want to be in the San Diego Zoo, or the one in Calcutta?

I had two stints of living in China between 2005-2007. In my first stay, I lived in a building with several expats, many who became friends. Nearby, there was a long park where I would jog. I had a memorable and enjoyable time. On my second stay, I decided to move to the complete other side of Shanghai. I lived in a building where nobody knew me nor spoke English (I can say about ten words in Mandarin to this day). The view out my window was an unbroken expanse of dull gray concrete. A combination of subway lines was necessary to get to any substantial park. I quickly fell into a deep funk. I had, unwisely, moved into a corner of the zoo that did not resemble my natural habitat. No community. No nature.

The conscious traveler has seen aspects of human zoos done better and worse around the world. Consider:

> In Indonesia, a joint of marijuana could get you a decade in prison. 20,000 Filipinos have died due to anti-drug enforcement. Over a million Americans were arrested for possession in 2020. Consumption has not decreased one iota since the "War on Drugs" was introduced almost 50 years ago. It seems to be effective only in ruining lives and decimating communities (specifically, underprivileged ones). We have forgotten the lessons from our long experiment with alcohol prohibition. Or maybe it was never about morality and public health…

On the other hand...

Portugal decriminalized all 'drugs'[11] in the year 2000. They took the money that went into penal systems and reallocated it to public health. Now, anyone with a problem receives therapy instead of punishment. Since implementing the policy, overdose deaths dropped by 80%; drug-related HIV infections by 90%.

❯ In many of the world's cities, one must purchase single use plastic bottles to get a clean drink of water.

On the other hand...

Portland, Oregon and Rome offer plenty of fresh drinking water to their citizens though ubiquitous fountains.

❯ In the typical American metropolis (and Jakarta) the automobile is strictly necessary for mobility. You see your fellow citizens surrounded by metal enclosures (and often outraged by the traffic).

On the other hand...

In most European cities (and Singapore) large portions of the town are delegated for pedestrian traffic. Long walkways connect citizens to a variety of pleasant plazas and parks, where they can witness their fellow humans at ease and play.

---

[11] It's often been said that we need a new vocabulary here. The term "drugs" is an extremely wide umbrella. Clearly alcohol, aspirin, magic mushrooms, and meth are all different animals (though the first is by far the biggest killer). Michael Pollen in his book *This Is Your Mind on Plants*, identifies the world's most popular drug as a stimulant. 90% of the world dabbles with caffeine.

The more you travel, the more constructs of the zoo you'll be exposed to. Take note of how you feel inside these differences. What is it that makes a place more livable? What is the secret sauce that gives a town a good vibe? Maybe it has something to do with the number of parks, gardens, pedestrian walkways, flowing water, support for the arts, and efficient public transportation. Maybe it's a government that allows you to lead your life as you wish, as long as you do no harm to others.

As you travel, consciously catalog the aspects of a better society. When you choose a future home, you'll know what to look for. Or, when you improve the place you call home, you'll know what to add. Whatever shape this environment takes, the ultimate goal is a happy you inside a happy community.

IKIGAI

"Hurry," said Sebastiaan as he hooked the manhole cover with a crowbar and slid it aside. The street, in the middle of Paris, was momentarily quiet. No cars coming, nobody entering or exiting the convenience store a few strides away. I scampered down into the abyss below the pavement on an iron ladder, followed by one of his assistants. We stood at the bottom for a moment, waiting for the Vampire King to follow. I turned on my headlamp and took a look around. We were in a white tunnel full of thick electrical wires.

"Sebastiaan," the assistant called out, looking up nervously at the open manhole above us.

"Shhh!" I said, motioning for quiet. I heard another voice now. It was faint, but even in the flowery language of French, there was the distinct tint of authority.

The assistant looked at me with concern. "I should go up," he suggested.

"No," I countered, "We should move."

Now I was sure that Sebastiaan was being questioned and was intentionally dragging the conversation out. He was stalling for us.

We hustled down the white tunnel until we came to a rupture in the side wall. It was just big enough to slither through. The assistant disappeared inside of it. I grabbed onto the sides of the hole and wiggled through. On the other end, my meager headlamp beamed feebly into an entirely different, and vast, environment.

We were now in the famous Parisian catacombs. Not the 2 kilometers they had curated for tourists, but the almost 200 km of ancient passageways and chambers that only a handful of savvy explorers knew how to (illegally) access. The city's police force ran a weekly patrol, but it covered a paltry portion of the expanse. For all intents and purposes, this was the wild west hiding directly below the civilized world. Anything could happen down here.

We scurried through a series of limestone passages and then hunkered down in a small room off to the side. I heard the distant sound of voices as we hid in the pitch dark. After almost 30 minutes a light came towards us. Just one light. It tracked right to the room. There was Sebastiaan, the Vampire King.

The police had arrived right after I descended. They only saw Sebastiaan on the street, hunched over the open manhole. He said he was alone. He found the cover open and was looking down out of curiosity. Then he went to another entrance to find us.

The rest of the story picks up on Road Less Traveled. We conducted a bizarre ritual in a room where the Knights Templar once gathered. They gave me a vampire name. You could say it was a unique experience.

The point of the story is really about who more than what. That is, who were all these people avoiding cops, sneaking through ancient catacombs, and engaging in ghoulish rituals? At this time of the night most folks were socializing in bars, or, more likely, at home in front of their televisions. How did this clan get lucky enough to have this super cool experience? The answer is: The Vampire King.

Father Sebastiaan, as he was known to the group, was once a young man fascinated with the vampire mythos. He went to dental school to learn how to make those pointy canines, becoming an excellent "fangsmith." Clever maneuvering ensued. Every soul who got a custom pair of fangs, was initiated into the Sabertooth Clan. Once you were in the group, you got special invitations, including an annual multi-day party in an Austrian castle.

Many of the members of the group were folks that seemed like they'd be outliers in mainstream culture. Most of them probably heard the labels nerd, geek, outcast, freethinker, introvert, eccentric, oddball, weirdo, character, and many other names used to describe folks who are passionate about fringe ideas. Perhaps, in their public schools and neighborhoods, few people understood them. However, one guy, following his passion, created a tribe to which they could *belong*. This particular night in the catacombs, nobody in Paris was doing anything as memorable as the shenanigans of the Saber-tooth Clan.

Father Sebastiaan did an excellent thing for himself, but, more importantly, he did something remarkable for hundreds, and now thousands, of people. He connected them to a community.

In commercial culture, we are trained to spot wealth by certain accouterments: The watch, the car, the yacht, the mansion. These are the signs that you've "made it". Many chase these material objectives in hope of some kind of fulfillment. Advertising naturally feeds this flame. The traveler, meeting people on every part of the economic spectrum, eventually sees through the smoke. It becomes undeniably easy to recognize the wealthiest people.

Let me tell you about a few I have met:

Kotch Voraakhom - An architect who believes the world has enough shopping malls. She is putting her effort into repairing the relationship between the citizens of Bangkok and water. Her projects clean up long-neglected canals and place lovely, green paths beside them. Folks now have new spaces to walk their dogs, play with their kids, and fall in love. Kotch is financially sound, respected, and sleeps contently at night. Every project makes her city just a little more clean and green, while improving the well-being of all citizens (rich or poor).

Edwin Weik - Founded the Wildlife Friends Foundation that rescues animals from captivity and brings them to a large refuge for rehabilitation. Tourists can stay at lodges and view elephants in a large pasture. Travelers volunteer. Edwin has a beautiful home at the refuge. He's financially sound, able to give employment to many, and beloved by the community.

Chris Brown - The owner of Reef Seen in northern Bali. While there are many dive shops on the island, this one is different. Chris has a vision for both the environment and community. He began projects to restore damaged reefs. He pays local fishermen to bring him turtles that get caught in nets (which previously would have been slaughtered). He started a turtle sanctuary. Tourists pay money to visit the sanctuary and release baby turtles into the ocean. That money goes back to the local fishermen and to fund community events. The whole village gathers on weekends to watch performances that happen on a stage he built. Chris is financially sound and able to spread opportunity. He is healing the natural environment and is beloved by the community.

Have you met people like this in your travels? People who have financial stability. People who are maximizing their talents. People who are admired and embraced by a community. People who can rest well knowing they are serving a good purpose. These people show the traveler a model for an actualized life. It's a model the traveler would be wise to ponder. How can we, also, find this sweet spot?

The Japanese have a name for this harmony: Ikigai.

Ikigai

A JAPANESE CONCEPT MEANING "A REASON FOR BEING"

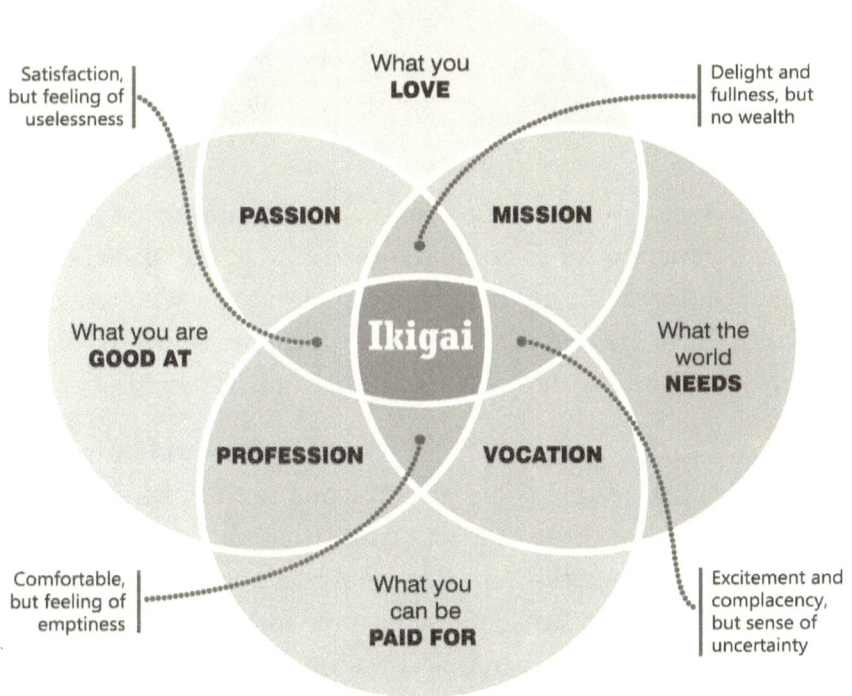

Satisfaction, but feeling of uselessness

Delight and fullness, but no wealth

What you LOVE

PASSION

MISSION

What you are GOOD AT

Ikigai

What the world NEEDS

PROFESSION

VOCATION

Comfortable, but feeling of emptiness

Excitement and complacency, but sense of uncertainty

What you can be PAID FOR

KISHORE B/SHUTTERSTOCK.COM

WHAT A CHARACTER!

I met Luuk in Rishikesh, India. The town is known as the birth-place of Yoga. It's full of Ashrams. If you are an established guru, you are revered here. If you are a wannabe guru, this is where you can gather the first of your flock. The town was full of people like Luuk and I, seeking answers to the meaning of life.

Luuk is a real character. Because his ideas diverge so far from the mainstream, few people really get to know the man. This is the curse of a divergent personality. If you are uber famous, like Jim Carrey, your peculiar perceptions don't cost you as much. If you are a regular joe, it's harder to find solidarity. Luuk had many ideas that were too woo-woo for my taste. But, every once in a while, he'd floor me with a deep perspective.

Luuk had met a woman at an airport a few months prior. They hit it off while waiting for their flights. The rub was, she turned out to be married. It was an arranged marriage to a man who struggled with alcohol, drugs, and gambling. The woman was unhappy in this union but was unsure of how to proceed. Luuk had an idea.

He started a dialogue with the wayward husband. He explained the whole situation, including his attraction to this man's wife. He bought a ticket for the man to come to Rishikesh and arranged for accommodation at an ashram that would help with detox and re-hab. As Luuk explained it, because he cared for the woman, and she cared for the absent husband, he would help the struggling man. Once the guy was up to speed, the woman could make her own choices on how to proceed.

I was by Luuk's side one day when the husband called to say he had missed his flight into Rishikesh for the second time. A flight Luuk had bought for him. The husband was heavily intoxicated. Luuk gently talked him through a game plan to get on the plane the next day. I'd never seen anything like it. How many people have the capacity to get into the messy mire of life like that?

The conscious traveler has met characters like Luuk before. The interesting outliers who have resisted the pressure to conform to mainstream choices. Months and years after the journey, these are the people that the traveler remembers. It's the authenticity that makes them memorable.

CHUNKY MONKEY

The truth is, we are all characters. Scratch the surface of your neighbor and you'll find some kink, some weird, and a little eccentric. Vanilla really isn't everyone's favorite flavor, although that's what we all talk about. We are afraid of how others would react if we mentioned the yumminess of spumoni, tutti frutti, or chunky monkey. The character, therefore, is brave. It takes courage to be authentic. But why?

Tara Brach, in *Radical Acceptance*, speaks about two wings, both essential for metaphorical full flight. One wing is clear-seeing. The other is holding our experience with compassion. Being seen and being loved are what we most deeply desire, but they must go hand in hand.

If we are loved, but not fully seen, it's hard to trust that love. There will always be the lingering thought, "If they really knew *this* about me, that love would evaporate." It would seem, however, that the inverse is worse. To be seen completely and then not loved is a nightmare scenario. Think about the times you poured your heart out to a lover who soon dumped you. That's real heartbreak territory. So many of us hold back portions of our true self for fear of rejection. If the fake cookie-cutter persona is rejected, it's not nearly as painful. Unfortunately, the cookie-cutter can't ever be fully loved. What a conundrum!

Characters have taken the leap. They are out there for the full package: complete acceptance or rejection. It ain't easy, but most things of value take effort and risk to attain. Here is a common journey of the character compared to the person wearing a social mask (for simplicity, we'll call them the (social) actor).

THE CHARACTER	THE ACTOR
Often the black sheep of the family. Maybe heard dad say, "Why can't you be more like your brother/sister."	Avoided drama with the family by adjusting to social cues. Any unusual interests or kinks were hidden at the first sign of disapproval.
Is often teased at school and always remembered.	Avoids social ridicule by blending in at school. Is easily forgotten.
Moves into a new town as an adult and is quickly known as the "crazy guy" or "eccentric girl." Most folks are scared that the character will drag them into an uncomfortable conversation, or ask a scary question, so they keep their interactions brief.	Moves into a new town and makes friends through the normal social channels: Talking about sports, politics, work, people at the office, relationships (though not too revealing of inner vulnerabilities) and sex (though careful not to stray into anything which could be seen as deviant).

THE CHARACTER	THE ACTOR
Slowly, other authentic and intellectually curious souls begin to befriend the character. They appreciate the insightful conversations the character is willing to have. Deep topics are often covered. The character and his friends open up into vulnerable terrain. Inside the expanding relationship, they feel seen, heard, and embraced.	Friendships plateau at a middling level. They rarely have challenging conversations which stress-test their beliefs or dig down into profound hopes and fears. They mostly stay on safer topics like sports, gossip, hobbies, and current events. Because no one makes themselves truly vulnerable, the actor questions if anyone else feels the way they do.
Supported by a strong tribe of other courageous individuals, the character does the work of their heart's calling. They become artists and innovators. They become the most kind, loving version of themselves. Their fearless self-compassion allows others to open up to their true nature.	Not fully seen or embraced, the actor stays in a job that seems comfortable. They often seek to buy things they hope will fill the void. The inner pain of their unmanifested self is numbed with drinking, busyness, overwork, and constant distraction. The impact they could make on society, or their social circle, is severely muted. Their dulled light does not give guidance to others on how to truly shine.

GETTING MESSY

In West Bengal, surrounded by plains of yellow mustard flowers, there is an obelisk commemorating a battle that changed India forever. Nearby, a plaque reads: "The British Force, led by Robert Clive, defeated Siraj-ud-Dollah, the Nawab (governor) of Bengal, Bihar, and Orissa. Nawab's soldiers were bribed by the British to throw away their weapons and surrender prematurely. Siraj was captured and brutally murdered. Thus, by promoting treason and forgery, the English force established their supremacy and the gruesome days of British rule began."

It's a clean narrative. The dirty imperial force vs. the golden local leader. But there are some things missing. The British force was financed by the elite bankers of Bengal. Locals. They paid the bribes. The mercenary who executed Siraj was also local.

Why would so many local people betray the governor? The answer is simple. Siraj was no King Arthur. Siraj was asking for it. In his book *Anarchy*, William Darrymple writes, "Not one of the many sources for the period - Persian, Bengali, Mughal, French, Dutch, or English - has a good word to say about Siraj. According to Jean Law, who was his political ally, 'His reputation was the worst imaginable.'" He insulted his generals, he physically assaulted the financial leaders, and, according to his own cousin, he was a cruel sexual predator.

We love a balanced story of good and evil: the Allies vs. Hitler, Xerxes vs. the Spartans, Darth Vader dueling with Luke, and Arnold defeating the predator. The problem is, these squeaky clean narratives can leave us feeling dirty. Let's forget Siraj and consider the people we admire.

Martin Luther King and John Kennedy had extra-marital affairs. Thomas Jefferson owned slaves. Ghandi had some troubling opinions about sex. Einstein was a cold husband. John Lennon was a bad father. The Spartans practiced infanticide.

None of these things can be washed away. It's not ok. Nonetheless, everyone on the list made great contributions to our world. They were all flawed heroes. In fact, if you dive deep into the nitty-gritty of anyone's life, things get messy. Statues and national anthems are clear, but real life is murky.

As a traveler, you will eventually notice this reality. At first, it might seem disheartening. Every time a culture finds someone to put on a pedestal, it turns out they walked on the same dirt as the rest of us. Eventually, the traveler will understand that there is no spotless savior. Then, they will find the empowering message within this fact.

If every hero was flawless, then you are disqualified from their ranks. You know all the terrible things you've done. You know how much you've let down the people you love. You know how you have failed to step up to your potential. If every hero is pure, you must be a bad person. There is no reason to try and rise up.

Understanding the messiness sets you free. It gives you permission to start again, right now. Degree by degree, you can turn the wheel of your ship to a new heading. Consider Frank Meeink, the former skinhead (and inspiration for the film American History X) who now dedicates his efforts to understanding and non-violence.

Faustin Ntiranyibagira, born in Burundi, was an abusive husband who now fights against domestic abuse in his community. Ric O'Barry trained captured dolphins to entertain humans. Now he leads the Dolphin Project and was named a Green Game Changer by the Huffington Post.

Life is messy. Everyone who is in the game, is in the muck. The conscious traveler knows that the path to something great isn't down the yellow brick road, but through the muddy, windy track. Heros keep trudging forward, with dirt between their toes.

THE HERO AND THE TRAITOR

My sleep was troubled. Something felt wrong. Too aggressive. We were on a bus traveling through the Ivory Coast by night. Dozing in my seat, I had not realized that the driver had spotted his buddy along the journey. Another bus driver en route. Now the two drivers, both young men, were racing each other down the dark highway. Suddenly, my friend yelled out in French.

"Do you think this is a game?! You are playing with our lives! Slow down!"

His commanding voice cut through a tension that had been gathering. Many passengers had become concerned, but were afraid of a confrontation with the driver. He had us less than three meters from the bumper of his friend's bus and moving at least 50 mph down a pitch black road.

The driver eased off the accelerator. My buddy shined a bright light on his bad behavior, and now it had to be acknowledged. We were immediately in a safer situation thanks to my friend's courage.

Have you seen the movie *300*? It loosely depicts the battle between a small group of Spartans (and Greek allies) versus a massive army of Persians (and their conscripts). The Greeks were led by King Leonidas. The Persians followed the orders of Emperor Xerxes. Although the Persians commanded many more soldiers, the Greeks had a clever technique to compensate for their numerical disadvantage: They squeezed the invaders into a tight pass. Only a handful of soldiers could stand side by side on this battlefield. The Spartans, who were better trained, more disciplined, and more motivated, began to massacre the Persian armies. Xerxes became demoralized as every day he sent troops into the meat-grinder with little success. The Greeks, who thought they were on a suicide mission, began to believe... maybe they could win this thing! Then, the worst kind of betrayal...

A local Greek herdsman, Ephialtes, agreed to show the Persians a secret trail that would lead behind the Spartan's position. He sold out his people for a sack of gold coins. When the news arrived at the Greek camp, Leonidas knew defeat was imminent. He allowed most of his army to flee. He would stay with the famous 300 Spartans, and a small group of other Greeks. They stayed to guard the retreat of the others. They stayed because there was a statement to be made. Surrounded from all sides, they were slaughtered. Their sacrifice (the ultimate sacrifice) changed the course of history.

A year ago, I stood on the spot where the Spartans made their last stand. My feet were planted where Leonidas bled to death from arrow wounds. I gazed up at the mountains beyond and imagined Ephialtes, the traitor, leading the Persians through them. What separated these two men? What roads did they take to arrive at heroic sacrifice and petty betrayal?

In his book, *12 Rules for Life*, psychologist Jordan Peterson suggests that the pursuit of selfish, impulsive pleasure is understandable. If life is full of tragedy and suffering, why not just get as much of the good stuff as you can? Cheat, lie, manipulate, deceive, intimidate, abuse… Whatever it takes to get what you want, when you want. The problem with this, to quote Peterson, is that "mere expedience, multiplied by many repetitions, produces the character of a demon. It's wrong because expedience merely transfers the curse on your head to someone else, or to your future self, in a manner that will make your future, and the future generally, worse instead of better."

This insight probably explains the character of Ephialtes. He was a dude who lived by the creed of expediency. He followed his impulses. He did not delay gratification. He sought the short-term benefit of any situation. He was the same kind of guy who would steal supplies from the office, take a handicapped parking spot, and leave his dog's doo-doo on the sidewalk. As he made all these small choices, he tried to always cover his tracks, so they wouldn't catch up to him. But, they always do. He may have rearranged mom's cookies so that it didn't seem like any were missing, but his soul couldn't be fooled. As Ephialtes always went for the easy and convenient option, he was molding his character. By the time he was an older man, and the Persians dangled a sack of gold, did he have a choice? Had he not already programmed himself to be a scumbag?

Leonidas, on the other hand, had undergone a strict upbringing. Young men could not run amok and do as they pleased. At age seven they were turned over to the state. They entered a never-ending training that taught them to sit with hardship, to cooperate, and to sacrifice. They came to value the community more than their own lives. As Leonidas always leaned into the meaningful options, he was molding his character. By the time he was a grown man, and the Persians invaded Greece, did he have a choice? Was he not already programmed to be a hero?

The traveler will see many examples of heroes and traitors in their journeys. It would be a mistake to think they were just "bad" or "good" people. The lesson is in the understanding that they slowly formed, decision by decision, into the person they became. Harriet Tubman, who helped slaves escape through the underground railroad, made a series of different choices than a prison guard in one of Stalin's gulags. One person took on risk to do what was right. Another avoided risk by doing what was wrong. The big choices came at the end of a long chain of smaller ones… all gaining momentum in different directions.

It's important to understand that history has remembered these characters as a lesson for you. These diverging roads continually roll out in front of us. That sack of gold would feel as good in your hand as it did in Ephialtes'. It would be so easy to say, "The Persians are going to win anyway. I may as well make a little money while I have the opportunity." Every CEO who dumps toxic waste into the water supply must repeat a similar line. Every arms dealer must think in similar patterns. "The world is already fucked, so I'll just get mine while I can." Remember, the traitor always starts with the small steps: Your bag of potato chips blows off the picnic table and ends up deep in a bush. It's a hassle to pick it up. The mountain already has trash on it. If the locals don't care, why should you?

Leonidas, like you and I, was always going to die. He could have fled the battlefield and gained a few more years of life. Instead, he continued a streak of meaningful choices with the ultimate one. Thousands of years later, he still inspires. Greek soldiers battling Nazi Germany took inspiration from the Spartan.[12] History honors Leonidas' choices to this day. He is the archetype of a hero. Remember, the hero always starts with the small steps: The bus driver is going too fast and texting. You don't speak the local language well. You suspect the guy is going to get angry if you call him out. He could even kick you off the bus. On the other hand, he's putting everyone's life at risk. Will you take a small Leonidas step and be a champion for the passengers, or is that not worth the unpleasantness of a confrontation?

Ponder this:

- How could you create changes in your home/neighborhood/community to make it a more human-friendly zoo?

- How close are you to having ikigai? What pieces of the graph are you missing and how could you take steps in that direction?

- Is there any aspect of your personal messiness that has been holding you back from moving towards greatness? Could you forgive yourself (and ask forgiveness of others), let it go, and begin again?

- Today, could you detect the small choices you make and determine if they lead down the road of Leonidas or Ephialtes?

---

[12] The battle of the Metaxas line holds many similarities to Thermopylae. At Fort Rupel the Greeks, outnumbered, forced the Germans into a narrow pass. When the Persians asked Leonidas to give up his weapons, he famously replied, "Come and get them." When the Nazi's asked Lieutenant Colonel Georgios Douratsos to surrender his position, he said, "The forts are not designed to be surrendered, but must be conquered."

You, the observant traveler, have seen, country by country and city by city, many different constructs of the human zoo. You have compared and contrasted. You carry this information to the place called "home" in an effort to change it for the better.

You, the seasoned traveler, have met thousands of people in your journeys. The ones you remember are the most authentic. The ones you learn to admire are in the eye of the ikigai: utilizing their full power, serving their community, and pursuing deep meaning with their choices. You have begun to ponder what your own life would look like in such wonderful harmony.

You, the mindful traveler, realize that this sweet spot of self-actualization cannot be rushed or forced. Instead, it's like a string of prayer beads that constantly runs through your fingers. Every heroic person you have met is like another bead on the chain. If you hold the question long enough, without demanding an answer, one will come. In the meanwhile, you are faced every day, in a spectrum of situations, with a choice: Do the expedient thing, or the meaningful one? Decision by decision you will mold your character. One day, when a big challenge arrives, this string of choices will determine if you step up, heroically; or cave and do the cowardly thing.

CONCLUSION

Strange... So many monkeys on this monolith.

I had just climbed a wearisome number of stairs to arrive at the summit of a massive rock pillar. Monkeys swung from the facade of a giant temple. A gaggle of priests sat in front. One man was reading the Ramayana into a microphone. Others banged on drums and blew into flutes. I walked through a dark passage leading into the shrine.

Inside, on a platform, a guru reclined on cushions. Surrounding him, a myriad of murals and statues made the purpose of this place clear. This was the home of the monkey god Hanuman, who joined Rama on his famous quest to rescue Sita (his wife) from Ravana (the demon king who had abducted her).

The guru gestured me forward.

"Do you have a question?" he asked.

I didn't, but I thought of something quickly.

"I heard that, in Hindu mythology, a person is renewed every seven years. Like they become a new..."

The man raised a finger to silence me. He held the pause, and then said, "Every breath."

"Ask one more question," he said, staring at me with a twinkle in his eye.

"Ok... uh... what's a lesson I can take from this story in the Ramayana?"

The man rose up to a seated position and crossed his legs. He leaned slightly towards me.

"Hanuman and the monkey army joined Rama on the quest to recover Sita... to reunite what was separated."

I nodded.

"The pantheon of the Hindu gods inhabited the bodies of the monkey soldiers for this mission. This is to say, when your purpose is true and righteous, the entire energy of the universe comes behind you. Do you understand?"

I nodded again, thanked the man, and left.

I've been unpacking this tiny moment for almost a dozen years. I think the guru was saying there is an eternal cosmic play unfolding. It's a story of separation and connection. The hero, finding their iki-gai, is on a mission to bring a broken corner of the world together in a more beautiful and harmonious way. There is something about this kind of mission that the universe finds pleasing. It's like hitting a baseball with the sweet spot of the bat, or nailing the high notes of a national anthem so that the audience is brought to tears.

You, the transformed traveler, are like the mythical Rama: Someone who is a connector in a divided world.

You've become a centered person through the deep experiences you've had on the road.

You've learned not to give your energy and resources away to people who are not ready to change. Instead, you focus them where change is possible.

You know how to spot the friendly helpers and close out the bad actors.

You understand your mortality, and that there is no time to waste.

You don't demonize others, but seek to understand them and find the commonalities.

You have an empowering belief system that is always open to positive adjustments and amendments.

You authentically bare your beating heart to the world.

You strive to make the right choices, even in the small things, rather than the easy ones.

The world has transformed you and now you are able to transform your world.

ACKNOWLEDGEMENTS

Mom and Dad, thanks for your constant support. My life assuredly went in different directions than you had anticipated, but you never showed disappointment with my choices. Everything has been easier knowing you were there.

Jess, thanks for your encouragement. Nobody embodies "hustle" more than you. It's extremely motivating to see your sibling crushing it.

Sashi, if you hadn't given me the opportunity to host *The Road Less Traveled*, this book would be a lot shorter. You've followed me into the belly of the beast quite a few times, my friend. I appreciate the constant vote of confidence and the good humor we pull out of the booms and busts. And you do it all with no susuk… unbelievable!

Eric, thanks for all the personal work you've done and shared. Thanks for seeing me. The concepts of life being messy and time being sacred had their inception in our vulnerable conversations.

Diana, thank you for your go-getter inspiration, the advice, and the emotional support. The perspective of a centered, kind-hearted, and powerful woman is priceless.

Greg, the concept of deeper vs. farther I first heard in a conversation with you. You are certainly a sterling example of a man who listened to the road and was transformed by it.

Armando, your drive to improve a little corner of the world, through media and education, constantly inspires me. Thanks for keeping me accountable.

James Dilworth, thanks for the moon ritual idea. Sitting down for tea with you, with your decimated Jeep still warm beside us, was critical to getting out of that high desert. That moment really cemented the principle of staying calm in the face of disaster. We have rehearsed that scenario many times! I cherish all those misadventures.

James Healthcote, thanks for sharing those first backpacking journeys with me. The hardest part of getting on the road is the first few steps. It sure helps to have a buddy willing to take the dive.

Jelena Stankovich, I've been able to go deeper in Serbia than any other European destination largely thanks to your support. Thanks for your positivity, hustle, and belief in my projects.

Anastasia Karachisarli, you've helped me immensely to go deep in Greece. Love your perspectives!

Chad Whiteman, thanks for that memorable time in Africa. Your courage to call that guy out stuck with me. If you ever get down in life, remember: You will improve with training.

Thanks to the Japanese director who pulled me aside on set. In a nutshell, he said, "It's time to die to your Tokyo life so your L.A. life can be born." He was a friendly helper extraordinaire.

Thank you to the travel writing OGs who provided much wanderlust. Pico Iyer and Tim Cahill jump to mind.

Thanks to the fans of *The Road Less Traveled* who have reached out to share some kind words. A lot of the messages get spammed, but I do eventually see them. I'm sorry that I haven't had the time to respond to every one of you. It warms my heart to know that something has resonated with you. When I speak into the camera, I try to speak straight to you with honesty, respect, and humility.

And finally, thanks to all the people I have met on the road who took the time to share a conversation with me. There have been thousands of small moments (like the Brad Pitt one mentioned in this book) which lifted my spirits, gave me something meaty to contemplate, and helped me become a better version of myself.

ENDNOTES

AHA 1

Singer, Michael A, and Institute Of Noetic Sciences. 2013. *The Untethered Soul : The Journey beyond Yourself.* Oakland, Ca: Noetic Books, Institute Of Noetic Sciences, New Harbinger Publications, Inc.

Campbell, Joseph. 1968. *The Hero with a Thousand Faces.* Princeton (N.J.): Princeton University Press.

Campbell, Joseph, Bill D Moyers, and Betty S Flowers. 2012. *The Power of Myth.* Turtleback Books.

AHA 2

Moore, Robert, and Doug Gillette. 2014. *King, Warrior, Magician, Lover : Rediscovering the Archetypes of the Mature Masculine.* HarperOne.

Clear, James. 2018. *Atomic Habits.* Penguin Publishing Group.

Sam Harris, discussion with Jonathan Kay, Quillette Podcast, Podcast Audio, March 25, 2022, https://quillette.com/2022/03/25/sam-harris-on-islam-dropping-acid-joe-rogan-vaccine-pseudoscience-the-wonders-of-meditation-collaborating-with-ricky-gervais-and-the-myth-of-free-will/.

AHA 3

Housel, Morgan. 2020. *The Psychology of Money : Timeless Lessons on Wealth, Greed, and Happiness*. Hampshire, Great Britain: Harriman House.

René Girard. 1992. *The Scapegoat*. Baltimore: Johns Hopkins University Press.

Jennifer Jones-Patulli. "Why We Hate Others." 2017. Hsdinstitute.org. 2017. https://www.hsdinstitute.org/resources/Why_we_hate_others.html.

Watts, Alan. n.d. *The Mythology of Hinduism*.

AHA 4

Gavin De Becker, and Tom Stechschulte. 2000. *The Gift of Fear*. Prince Frederick, Md: Recorded Books.

Brach, Tara. 2004. *Radical Acceptance : Embracing Your Life with the Heart of a Buddha*. New York ; Toronto: Bantam Dell.

AHA 5

Burgis, Luke. 2021. *Wanting : The Power of Mimetic Desire in Everyday Life*. New York: St. Martin's Press.

Twist, Lynne, and Teresa Barker. 2017. *The Soul of Money : Reclaiming the Wealth of Our Inner Resources*. New York: W.W. Norton & Company.

AHA 6

Becker, Ernest. 1973. *The Denial of Death*. London: Souvenir Press, , Cop.

Burkeman, Oliver. 2022. *Four Thousand Weeks*. Random House Uk.

Shelley, Percy Bysshe. "Ozymandias." *Poetry Foundation*, 2020, https://www.poetryfoundation.org/poems/46565/ozymandias

Kabat-Zinn, Jon. 2004. *Wherever You Go, There You Are*. London: Piatkus.

Wasson, Gordon. 1957. Review of *Seeking the Magic Mushroom*. *Life*, May 1957.

Mckenna, Terence. 1999. *Food of the Gods : The Search for the Original Tree of Knowledge : A Radical History of Plants, Drugs and Human Evolution*. London: Rider.

Muraresku, Brian. 2020. *The Immortality Key : The Secret History of the Religion with No Name*. New York: St. Martin's Press.

Andrew Huberman, Huberman Lab, Podcast Audio, April 18, 2022, https://hubermanlab.com/using-light-sunlight-blue-light-and-red-light-to-optimize-health/

AHA 7

Ryan, Christopher. 2019. *Civilized to Death : The Price of Progress*. New York: Avid Reader Press.

Pollan, Michael. 2021. *This Is Your Mind on Plants*. New York: Penguin Press.

Brach, Tara. 2004. *Radical Acceptance : Embracing Your Life with the Heart of a Buddha*. New York ; Toronto: Bantam Dell.

Dalrymple, William. 2020. *ANARCHY : The Relentless Rise of the East India Company*. S.L.: Bloomsbury Publishing.

Peterson, Jordan B. 2018. *12 Rules for Life : An Antidote to Chaos*. Toronto: Vintage Canada.

ABOUT THE AUTHOR

Jonathan Legg has hosted 5 seasons of The *Road Less Traveled*, exploring off-the-beaten-path destinations worldwide. He produced and directed *Food Relay*, and appeared on *Fear Island: Fortress of the Bears*. When not filming he can be found leading small groups on adventures, flying a paraglider, and helping young men find their own empowering stories and purpose.

Find out more @ Jonathanlegg.com

www.Ingramcontent.com/pod-product-compliance
Lightning Source LLC
Chambersburg PA
CBHW020240130626
46549CB00005B/1992